ELAINE FEINSTEIN

Elaine Feinstein has long been admired as the author
of novels which crystalise the European drama of this
century. She is also a poet, the translator of THE
SELECTED POEMS OF MARINA TSVETAYEVA, and a
dramatist who has worked for both radio and tele-
vision. She was made a Fellow of the Royal Society of
Literature in 1980, awarded the Cholmondeley Prize
for poetry in 1990, and made an honorary Doctor of
Letters at the University of Leicester in the same
year. Elaine Feinstein is married, with three sons, and
lives in London.

'Elaine Feinstein's treatment of Brecht is memorable, especially the grip he exerted on so many of his lovers . . . she has a sophisticated understanding of what it is that makes his chauvinism so attractive. And it is this subtlety of characterisation that makes Frieda's tale paticularly engrossing'

The Daily Telegraph

'The novel's trump card is its vivid, sketchy narration, believable precisely because it captures the imperfect, impressionistic quality of memory'

Literary Review

'Elaine Feinstein is one of our best poets, and she knows about the way words work, how they can carry more force and wisdom than appearances on the surface. Her reader needs to be alert and open, and will be richly rewarded'

Evening Standard

'Elaine Feinstein writes with her customary grace, poise and pain'

The Observer

'Frieda's tragic childhood is described in spare, brilliant prose'

The Times

Elaine Feinstein

LOVING BRECHT

For Adam, Kate, Lara and Katriona

Copyright © Elaine Feinstein 1992

First published in Great Britain in 1992 by Hutchinson

Sceptre edition 1993

Sceptre is an imprint of Hodder and Stoughton Paperbacks, a division of Hodder and Stoughton Ltd

The author is grateful to John Fuegi for the use of his forthcoming book *Brecht and Co: An Archaeology of Voices* from which she has greatly benefited. John Fuegi's research has uncovered material which throws important new light on the extent to which Brecht took the work of his talented female collaborators, such as Elizabeth Hauptmann and Margarete Steffin.

British Library C.I.P.

A CIP catalogue record for this title is available from the British Library

ISBN 0-340-58475-0

The characters and situations in this book are entirely imaginary and bear no relation to any real person or actual happenings.

The right of Elaine Feinstein to be identified as the author of this work has been asserted by her in accordance with the Copyright, Designs and Patents Act 1988.

This book is sold subject to the condition that it shall not, by way of trade or otherwise, be lent, re-sold, hired out or otherwise circulated without the publisher's prior consent in any form of binding or cover other than that in which it is published and without a similar condition including this condition being imposed on the subsequent purchaser.

No part of this publication may be reproduced or transmitted in any form or by any means, electronic or mechanical, including photocopying, recording or any information storage or retrieval system, without either the prior permission in writing from the publisher or a licence, permitting restricted copying. In the United Kingdom such licences are issued by the Copyright Licensing Agency, 90 Tottenham Court Road, London W1P 9HE.

Printed and bound in Great Britain for Hodder and Stoughton Paperbacks, a division of Hodder and Stoughton Ltd, Mill Road, Dunton Green, Sevenoaks, Kent TN13 2YA. (Editorial Office: 47 Bedford Square, London WC1B 3DP) by Clays Ltd, St Ives plc.

PART ONE

BERLIN

'For this bleak existence
Man is seldom bad enough.'

Brecht: 'Song of the Inadequacy of Human Endeavour'

1

My name is Frieda Bloom.

If some of you recognize that name, or find a tune of Kurt Weill starting up in your head as you hear it, it is because I worked with Bertolt Brecht in the Twenties, and the smoke of Berlin cabaret hangs around me even now.

These days I often dream of the huge square house in Charlottenberg where I was born. It is not an unhappy dream. Upstairs are my Aunt Clara and an English nursemaid who helped my mother; and downstairs dark cool rooms where jars of bottled fruit were stored, their lids sealed by rubber bands.

On the shiny black piano stood a photograph of a delicate child standing on ballet points; her shoes ribboned. The photograph was hand-tinted to bring out the pink on the elfin cheeks and the bow at the waist of the organdie dress. Her hair fell without a curl down to her waist. It was a photograph of my sister, who died before I was born, and whose pretty ghost continued to haunt the household.

Almost my earliest memory is of that English nanny tugging her comb through my bristly black hair and grumbling, 'Your hair is too thick. Like an animal or an African.'

'People used to stop and look at you in your pram,' my mother would say, suggesting things had changed sadly since those days.

Everything had changed for the worse, I knew, as soon as I stopped being a simple adjunct of her own perfection. Generously, she continued to dress me in a white coat and gloves, and frowned to see my olive skin glowing almost green by contrast.

'She takes after her father's family,' she would say, with a little sniff of disapproval which included the only member of that family I knew, namely Aunt Clara.

It was upstairs in Aunt Clara's room I sometimes wept.

'I wish I was Minna,' I said, meaning my dead sister.

'Poor Minna,' said Aunt Clara vigorously. She was a big-boned woman who usually dressed in surprisingly shiny clothes because she had once kept a dress shop, and after its failure had brought a good deal of stock to hang in our capacious wardrobes. 'You need not envy her.'

'She was pretty,' I said. My own features were strong and straight, but my face was too long, and my eyes too dark.

'Pretty enough,' conceded Clara, 'but she's gone, hasn't she?'

Clara had a wonderfully light way with dance steps for someone of such heavy build. I was probably the only six-year-old girl who could dance an intricate foxtrot.

'Let me show you how to dance the way men will like it,' she would say. 'A woman can always get a man if she knows how to follow.'

My father himself was a handsome man with huge and mournful eyes, and a lopsided smile. Life, I always understood, had disappointed him, and he had not become the man he wanted to be.

'I might have been a lawyer,' he sometimes said. 'I might have done anything.'

And his mournful brown eyes turned on my mother thoughtfully.

'He adored Minna,' my mother would mutter then, as if that adoration had for a time been enough to ward off the unhappiness in those eyes.

'He took the easy way,' Aunt Clara would say energetically.

'Father left him a thriving business. Why should he grumble?'

But I knew there was something sadder in his soul than she understood. Some nights he came into my room after I had fallen asleep, and sat on my bed. When he saw that I was awake, he said huskily, 'I'm so unhappy. Sing for me, Frieda, like Minna did.' Even then, though, something in his urgency made me nervous. I sang in tune but whatever I sang he wept. He would not let me stop, but simply sat there crying for his lost child.

4

In the lilac room, which was hardly ever used, I sometimes imagined a happier world, to which I had access through the tiled fireplace. Beyond it were armies ready to respond to the slightest call of my voice. I could summon them by speaking through the many-coloured abalone shell that lay on the mantelpiece, and sometimes I spoke my secret dreams into that shell, and I listened for an answer.

I asked my mother once where Clara's husband had gone, and afterwards I heard my mother and father talking together about the question, which seemed to disturb them.

'I hope you told her he has gone to heaven, as if talking to a Christian child?' my father asked vigorously.

I knew I was not a Christian child, but something else, something which took the family twice a year to a building lit with shimmering candles intended to suggest the presence of the Living God. There I sat in the balcony, looking down, clothed in my best white coat, with a light perspiration on my back. Release only came when the moment arrived for prayers to be said for the dead. Then all the children were sent outside and I stood with chattering cousins from my mother's family. And even that brought its own embarrassment. Somehow I, who had been bathed so completely from head to toe, felt ugly and sweaty while the other children romped and played. I couldn't do that. Sometimes I tried very hard and brought out a single, eccentric thought which temporarily silenced them.

'She's swallowed the dictionary,' one of my cousins would say.

And then at the end we would get solemnly into my father's car (it smelled of wood and polish) which had been discreetly parked out of sight of the entrance to the synagogue, for a synagogue is what it was.

We had Christmas like everyone else. For some reason, my mother drew the line at a crib with a doll in it; but there were baskets of food and sweets everywhere; and a huge tree with golden angels, and coloured glass balls, and presents for everyone lying at its foot. I would come down early and watch the maid light the family stove. She would have a large mixing bowl on her knees, into which she dropped eggs and sugar and almonds, and I was allowed to scoop up the mixture greedily when the cake had been poured.

2

My father had inherited a considerable fortune from an eider-down-cleaning business, and had branched out successfully into the manufacture of gloves. The eiderdown-cleaning business had probably begun to founder even before the end of the war but when the glove-making industry collapsed too, he was ruined. So it was that we had to move from our comfortable house.

I cannot remember the hardships of our moving, but I do remember the small rooms on a third floor, in a very different part of Berlin. My mother put me to sleep on a wooden bed like a box, and gave me a sugar lump with hot milk to console me. Soon afterwards, she was sorting, ironing and arranging bundles of neighbours' laundry to pay the rent.

My father was inconsolable. He sat for hours at a time in his chair, unshaven, not always fully dressed, like a stunned and unhappy animal. The squalor of the house increased, and he grew savagely critical of our hopeless life. He was not meant for such conditions, he could not endure the dingy rooms in which he found himself, He longed for the house which had once been his. My mother smiled and made the best of it.

At first my father was reluctant to go to the tavern on the corner of our street. Some acquaintance from his former life must have taken him, and he came back cheerful. Soon he spent whole evenings there. When he came into my room after an evening at the tavern he was too sleepy to listen if I sang to him. Some nights he would rock on his chair and moan, so that I had to stop and clasp both arms around his neck, crying, 'Don't, don't, I love you so much.'

The first time he hit me was a complete surprise. I was sitting across the broken chair on which I had thrown my clothes when I got into bed, and my father perceived the untidiness with anger.

6

'No delicacy,' he snarled, and lunged at me like a bear. The blow grazed my mouth so that the lips caught my teeth. And when I put my hand up to my mouth I found it was bleeding. Incredulous tears came to my eyes. He was clearly horrified himself.

'Now don't you try and make me feel guilty,' he said angrily.

Nothing could have been further from my thoughts. I could only see the fault as mine. If I had been a delicate creature like Minna he would have loved me; I should have been able to sweeten his terrible fate. Instead I was only a constant reminder of the injustice life had been for him. I wept not for the blow, but because I wanted to be perfect in his eyes and to make him happy, and both those things seemed impossible.

I don't know when my mother came into the room, but as I became aware of her presence what I felt was shame.

'I'm sorry,' I said, and ran to the bathroom.

I could hear my mother's plaintive voice behind me. 'What is the matter with the girl?'

In the bathroom I scrutinized my face. I saw with fascination that there was as yet no outward sign of the blow, but as I fingered my cheek, I observed that the flesh inside my mouth had swollen and darkened to the colour of uncooked liver.

I came back into the room much later with downcast eyes, hoping my mother would not question me. My father glared at me and came over to see what was wrong. I opened my mouth dumbly, and gestured at the liverish stain; he was horrified at once.

'My wonderful little girl,' he said. 'How brave of you not to complain or cry out.'

I received his words with a shy smile. Wonderful, he had called me wonderful. The happiness of that word suffused my whole body. I would have let myself be torn apart at the stake to earn that praise from him again.

His approval was so necessary to me. I didn't care about school work; in class I usually dreamed or scribbled bits of verse; silly verse for the most part, laced with rhymes and puns which made my friends laugh. My term reports declared me erratic, and I won no prizes at the end of the year. Even if I had, the only reward I wanted was some sign of my father's love.

7

I must have been nearly twelve when my Aunt Clara, who was living in a room of her own by now, came to supper. My father was out, and I did not listen to much of the conversation, but afterwards, while I was helping my aunt wash up, I began to voice some of the anxieties I now had.

'Tell me, Aunt Clara,' I asked, 'since you once said men would like me . . . Am I pretty? When I look into the mirror I'm not sure.'

And she turned to me with her lively, searching eyes and said with enormous kindness and total honesty, 'No, little Frieda, you are not exactly pretty. But men will like you just the same.'

My mother bought food on the black market; sometimes I went with her to the cafés where we could buy candles and potatoes in return for a few remaining silver spoons or some lacy dress from happier days. In Ma Reinicke's café, men with beards, whom my mother referred to nervously as gangsters, opened their suitcases on the scruffy tables, while an occasional policeman looked on indifferently.

It was in that café I first saw Wilhelm. The only reason I noticed him was because a girl, in a red slip scantily covering her thin body, came to join him, and while I watched he put his hand under her short skirt and took out a handful of money from the top of her stocking. He was little more than a gangling boy, but the money she handed over was a great deal, I perceived with surprise. I don't know what there was in the transaction to interest me, aside from the impudent confidence of the girl, but my intense gaze on Wilhelm made him aware of me. My stare often attracted people's attention and sometimes alarm. He looked around, feeling that gaze, but seeing I was no more than a twelve-year-old girl, gave me a weak and ingratiating smile.

'Gangsters,' my mother said nervously.

I thought I would rather like to be a gangster. Back home, in front of a mirror, I stood with a stolen cigarette sloping out of my mouth, and an expression which I imagined resembled that of the girl with the banknotes in her stocking.

One night there was an explosive quarrel between my mother and father. I don't know what occasioned it. I was sitting in the kitchen, scribbling on one of the maps that we had been given for our geography lesson, when I heard my mother begin to weep loudly. It was an unusual sound, since she was usually smiling and chirpy even late at night. Horrified, I opened the door and made out voices in the bedroom.

'I can't go on like this,' my father shouted. His voice was thick, but whether with anger or alcohol I could not be sure.

My heart was pounding as I approached the bedroom door, afraid to make my presence known.

'Nobody visits us any more.'

'It is August,' said my mother foolishly.

And then there was a sickening thud, and a gasp. I was so alarmed I rushed to open the door and stood before both of them as a witness. My father's eyes dropped before my angry gaze. My mother had her head lowered, and was tidying her clothes. She rose and took advantage of my presence to say calmly, 'I will set out the supper. Come and help me, Frieda.'

After eating, my father lay back in his chair and my mother fussed round him, doing her best as always to improve the situation.

'He is not well,' she defended herself from my raised eyebrows.

She brought him chicken soup and so forth, while he barked, 'Why must we live like this? We deserve better.'

'Things aren't so bad,' she said.

'You think this is a normal life?'

'This year,' my mother tried to say.

'People of sense don't slum like this,' he sneered. 'The whole world doesn't live in a slum.'

I worried for my mother as I stood in the kitchen drying the dishes she patiently washed.

'You must be tired,' I said, 'after working all day.'

'That's how it is,' she sighed.

I was more disturbed than this suggests. It was a hot night, and the thought of getting into bed seemed intolerable. My mother I heard going to her bed, where my father was already snoring, and I felt she was at least at peace for the night. Then I slipped out.

Our flat was on G . . . strasse, which gave on to one of those green spaces that Berlin enclosed inside itself. I had always been forbidden to enter that parkland after dark because strange people hovered there. The pain I felt in my heart at what I had seen made all other dangers seem remote. It was a night with a great moon, and as I walked out into the unlit spaces I was led by the sound of shallow water. I remembered there was a stream close by, running under a bridge, and soon I was standing there, looking at the moonlight where stones parted the water. The cool darkness of the trees reached into me. Altogether the beauty called to me like the tones of a plangent instrument voicing a melody I could not name, easing my spirit and confirming my sense that the greatest dangers were not in the unknown world, but in the world I found most familiar.

3

My father had begun to go out every evening and my mother no longer waited up anxiously for him. He came home a little the worse for drink, and usually fell into bed without disturbing either of us. One night, however, he appeared in my room, as if by mistake, and there was something in his face which I did not understand.

'Are you all right?' I asked.

'My dear girl,' he said hopelessly and put out his arms for an embrace. He looked very handsome and oddly happy. Almost without thinking I assumed the mothering position, with his big handsome face held against my breasts. He lay there for a time, sighing as I stroked his hair.

'What a good girl you are,' he said.

'Shall I sing for you?' I asked.

But he seemed to hear nothing, and I continued to cradle him to me, while he pushed his face deeper and deeper in the small hot mound of my left breast. A strong sour smell, of ill-digested brandy, made me draw my own face slightly away and the movement led him to clutch me to him.

'Don't,' I said involuntarily.

'My little girl,' he said. 'I won't hurt you.'

I began to feel faintly alarmed at the intensity of the pressure, and the bloated sleepiness of the face at my breast. I wriggled a little and the movement led him to change the position of his hands so that one now held my thigh while the other pushed under my nightdress as far as my knee.

'What are you doing?' I shrieked.

The noise appeared to waken him from whatever drunken dream possessed him, and his eyes opened to fix me with a stare of black hostility.

'You will walk the streets,' he said. 'You have the mind of a sewer creature.'

11

And, flinging me from him so roughly that I caught my head against the corner of the wardrobe, he got unsteadily to his feet and left me to my thoughts. I lay awake for a long time, my heart banging with fear. Gradually, as the silence confirmed he had gone to his own bed, the fear lessened and I was left mainly with a familiar feeling of shame. I felt no anger towards him, only a sense of my own uncleanliness.

The next morning I rushed to talk to my mother who was preparing breakfast and tried to explain what had frightened me. She seemed altogether concerned with her daily tasks.

'What nonsense you talk,' she said.

'You think I invented it?'

'An overheated imagination,' she muttered, and began to take off her apron and prepare her small leather bag for work.

'What shall I do if it happens again?' I begged her to tell me.

'It never happened,' she sighed. 'Please don't annoy me, Frieda.'

Her complacency convinced me during the hours of daylight, but at night I nevertheless decided to lock my door, and usually lay in bed shivering until I heard my father shuffle past in the direction of his room. Several nights went by in peace and I had begun to relax when, late one Saturday, I heard footsteps pause outside my room and the handle shake. At once, completely awake with terror, I sat bolt upright in my bed. The rattling stopped and was replaced by a low whisper.

'Frieda, open the door.' My father's voice was urgent and sad, but I lay where I was, shaking and silent.

The rattling began again, and he hit the door in his exasperation. 'You can't be so fast asleep,' he grumbled.

I lay silently where I was, hardly daring to believe that the lock would hold. Then my mother's sleepy voice called out in a puzzled way about the noise and my father called back some reassuring reply. Presently I heard the sound of his footsteps going away.

My mother had taken on a new job, and one day she needed me to go on my own and try to exchange six silver spoons for some flour and potatoes at Ma Reinicke's café. Dull with a sense of my own shame, I did as she asked. Before I had reached the tables where people gathered with shabby suitcases to barter matches, screws, anything, the young man I had seen a few weeks earlier came up to me, saying, 'Haven't I seen you before?'

I recognized him apathetically, and smiled.

'What do you do?' he asked me.

'I'm a schoolgirl,' I explained.

'Hm,' he said and his eyes examined me.

Hot blood came up into my cheeks as I remembered what my father had said of me. And yet I was not altogether sorry to be looked at in that way. I lifted my head as proudly as I could.

'If you ever want to go on the stage,' he suggested, 'come and see me.'

It was not an idea I had ever entertained before, but it pleased me instantly. I stood there for a moment intoxicated with the idea that Wilhelm found something in me people might applaud. That may sound romantic, but I was perplexed and lonely and I needed to value myself for something. His words transported me back to a world of my solitary childhood games in the lilac room with the Lalique glass and the abalone shells. And what I heard through those shells was not the sound of the sea, but the sound of applause. It lifted and floated me more tenderly than any wave. I cannot remember what I stammered then, as I collected the flour and potatoes, and refused his offer to carry them to my door, but I remembered his face and his words.

My mother received the flour and potatoes that I carried home that night with a certain churlishness which might have alerted me to what had happened. Instead I went up to my room without suspicion, and was alarmed to find my father already sitting there. He was coldly sober, dressed quite formally, with his hair well combed. His expression, however, was ugly.

'What lies have you been telling your mother?' he asked dangerously.

'No lies,' I stammered.

'You bitch,' he said. 'You make me out a monster? You should have more respect.'

13

To mollify him, I said, 'I was afraid. I only said I was afraid.'
My words seemed to madden him more.

'Afraid? I'll silence your filthy tongue.'

I saw then he had a leather belt in his hand and was binding it firmly round the palm of his right hand.

'Please!' I begged, incoherent with terror. 'Please.'

'You have to be taught a lesson,' he said.

4

That night I lay in bed with weals on my buttocks and a slight fever. What my mother said, or how she excused my father's behaviour, I have forgotten, but I understood that she could not protect me. Her eyes, behind glass now and faintly tinged with red, took on a pained expression of reproach.

In my own room I had a silver napkin ring which had been a gift of my Aunt Clara. In better times I had been impatient with it. In a house where napkins were washed by servants after use, it had no real function; and it was never set out now on the check lino cloth my mother used for most of our meals. I kept it in a drawer in my room.

At this distance of time I can't be sure whether it was a week or a month before I packed the napkin ring and a few clothes in a small case. I remember deciding to leave no note, as I set out from the home which now seemed more frightening than the streets.

Down the stairs and through the front door I went with my heart banging. It was a long walk to my aunt's flat. I had expected her to be living close by in circumstances worse than our own, since all my childhood my father had been a rich man and Clara a dependant. The street smelled sweet in the early morning. Autumn leaves cracked underfoot in the quiet. A horse and cart were making an early delivery to a glassware shop, and the head of the horse came round to inspect me with mild curiosity as I stepped through the delivered crates. Soon I found myself walking across Alexanderplatz into a neighbourhood with grand shop fronts.

As I paused to check the street name at the corner of a fine department store, a man with a heavy overcoat secured by string blocked my way and held out a begging tin. His face was purple, his breathing stertorous.

'I have nothing,' I said.

He rattled the tin impatiently.

I had taken as little money as I could from my mother's purse, since I knew she would be answerable to my father.

'Leave the child alone, you brute,' called a woman dressed in high boots from across the road.

'Shut your mouth, you whore,' he replied, turning away from me as I rushed past him into my aunt's block of flats.

A concierge sat in the mirrored entrance hall. He looked me over suspiciously as I read out the address I had, and retreated to another room to confirm by telephone that my aunt was willing to see me. As I rose to the sixth floor in a small lift, I inspected my scared, open eyes in the tinted mirror and understood why the concierge had hesitated. My aunt received me on the landing, hugged me to her with all the power of her huge muscled arms, and brought me into her apartment.

She was wearing a black Japanese housecoat, with a dragon embroidered over one shoulder, and she smelled of sandalwood soap. As she brought me into her kitchen, I looked around with surprise. Everything was magnificently appointed. There were jars of spices, towels in deep colours, and a fine copper and glass percolator into which she was putting spoons of unmistakably real coffee.

'Would you like croissants?' she asked.

I had not eaten other than the cheapest bread for so long that I gasped with delight and began to inspect her closely. She was certainly looking well. Her face was framed by black hair cut straight round her face and her mouth looked plump and red. She was a complete stranger to me.

The main living room of the flat was furnished with Bauhaus furniture in leather, steel and wood, but any severity was modified by signs of my aunt's occupation in the form of silk stockings thrown over chairs and a pretty pink slip on the floor. She gathered this carelessly, and left me looking into a cabinet with small ivory figures, engaged I saw in arcane sexual couplings.

'Is this your house?' I asked involuntarily as she came back with a tray.

She laughed. 'It belongs to a friend of mine,' she explained. 'A M. Barbusse, who is at the moment in Geneva.'

16

I drank the coffee and began to tell my story, which she listened to with nods and exclamations of horror.

'You won't tell my father where I am?' I asked.

'That brute,' she said angrily. 'I should like to give him a piece of my mind. But you needn't worry, I always knew how to keep my mouth shut.' And she mimed silence.

'What do you intend to do?'

'I don't know,' I said helplessly.

'Stand up,' she said.

I did so and her eyes wandered up and down my body. At length, she sighed, 'There are girls of twelve in the business these days. Well,' she murmured, and put an affectionate arm on my neck, 'I am sure we can find you a job as a waitress.'

'You seem to have prospered,' I ventured.

'Leaving your house was the best thing that ever happened to me,' she said dreamily. 'At the time it seemed a disaster, but it is often very difficult to tell good luck from bad. Sometimes what you fear most is best for you.'

I swallowed and promised to remember her words.

That night I lay on a soft mattress, breathing in odours of sandalwood so sweetly that I drowsed off to sleep without any problem. At three in the morning, however, I woke with a shock and made out the unfamiliar face of a luminous clock close to my pillow. I sat up then with a frenzy of confused emotions. I was still frightened that my father would seize me and drag me home; yet at the thought of being hidden away from him, waves of misery shook my body. I began to sob. Even as the gasps tore at me, I knew that I was not missing my poor mother, who no doubt already grieved for me. It was my father I missed. And not that strange father of the last hard months but another, half-remembered, childhood father who had once brought me gifts, listened to me sing and seemed to need me. I might be safe, but without his love I felt myself unloved and lonely. The loneliness permeated my whole being.

My grotesque sobs woke Aunt Clara who came to comfort me. I tried to explain what I was thinking, but she misunderstood my unhappiness. Again and again, she reassured me that my father

17

would never find me, while I struggled with the overwhelming knowledge of my loss.

The next morning my aunt tried to find me clothes to wear. I was less than helpful. I let her try one after another against my skinny frame, giggling with her at the difference in our shapes until at last she found something suitable for alteration. In no time she was down on her knees, tucking and gusseting with pins in her mouth, while I stood as still as I could with ungrateful impatience. Then off she scurried, while I sat eating toast and jam, listening to her sewing machine whirr from next door.

I had never worn green before, still less with a touch of gold lamé at the hip, and I was startled at my appearance in the mirror.

'I look like a showgirl,' I said, far from displeased. The creature I saw in the mirror had huge dark eyes, long legs, and something of the awkwardness of a newly born animal, like a foal or faun.

'Well, you are going to work in Trude Westerborg's,' said my aunt. 'I've arranged it. But you have to look right.'

I think I had been expecting a café rather like the one in which my mother and I bartered for household goods; a grey and ill-lit room, where poorly dressed men sat over their beer and sometimes put their heads down on the tables. In Trude Westerborg's cabaret there were fat men with cigars, bottles of champagne in silver buckets, women in flashing silks, their dresses cut to show their knees, held up by strings on their arms. Their hair was short, their breasts small and when a saxophone began to play they danced wildly. I was euphoric when I was told I could wait on the tables for a week's trial to see if I dropped soup and beer into the patrons' laps.

'You can stay with me for a bit,' said my aunt, though I could see she was a little worried about it. Her M. Barbusse was coming back at the end of the month from Geneva.

I was only fifteen and very frightened. Simply, I wanted to eat, sleep warmly, not to be harassed, not to go under.

Waiting at tables did not seem servile to Aunt Clara. This was because she thought good things might come of it. Most of the girls had boyfriends who collected them after work, and gave them a good time. Some girls lived with their families like me; others were pretty, slender-boned creatures who longed to be put into a chorus line in a show on the Ku'damm. One or two had husbands who were out of work, or children to support. None of them had much schooling.

I was clumsy with the dishes, but I coped well enough. As the evening wore on my legs ached, and I longed to be back in my aunt's flat being pampered with hot drinks. Once, about halfway through the evening shift, I felt so exhausted I burst out crying in the cloakroom, and sat there for a while smelling the dusty coats and oilcloth and snuffling in a fit of self-indulgence until one of the other girls, with a little cat face and sharp eyes, found me.

'What are you blubbering about?' she said, with an edge of spite.

I couldn't answer.

'You aren't living in Charlottenberg now,' she said. 'Dirty Jew.'

'I'm not,' I said.

'Not a Jew or not dirty?' she teased me.

I had no ready reply.

One day I unearthed a new typewriter at the bottom of my wardrobe, and brought it to my aunt with some excitement. She glared at it.

'Never learn to type,' she said with that flash of assertion which made her words so memorable to me. 'Why do you think men don't learn to do it?'

'Why do you have it here, then?' I asked.

'There's an instruction manual somewhere,' she said, beginning to investigate the cupboard with some energy. 'Take it if you like, but my advice is don't meddle with it.'

I can't remember when it was Wilhelm first made himself known to me again at Westerborg's. He caught my hand as I was clearing his table of beer glasses, and I was rather cross.

'I've seen you before,' he said. 'Not here. Across town.'

I remembered him of course, but I didn't particularly want to pursue the relationship. He looked surly and spoiled, and his

19

mouth was slack because he had been drinking all evening. He held my hand tight as several spotlights focused on Herr Baumann, also called Olympia the Tattooed Lady, who was beginning his act. Herr Baumann wore a flaming red wig. His large female body (made of papier-mâché) was stuffed into a skimpy two-piece costume.

'You can have a drink if I buy you one,' Wilhelm murmured, but though I had often seen girls drink with clients, the system of such encounters was regulated with some precision and had not been explained to me. I pulled away, saying as much, and he burst out laughing.

So I sat as he asked.

'Here at my rear,' declaimed Herr Baumann-as-Olympia, 'is a part of me that has attracted the particular interest of a high official in the Ministry for Arts and Letters.'

The crowd roared their approval of this and Wilhelm put a hand on my knee. I took it off again.

Herr Baumann was meanwhile showing the audience tattoos on his buttocks and thighs. 'I cannot show you absolutely everything,' he declared, 'as certain parts of my rear are under police edict.'

Wilhelm reclaimed my knee. 'You'd like to go on the stage, wouldn't you?' he asked, his voice slurred, and his eyes blinded with an expression that suddenly recalled my father.

I pulled away.

'All the girls want to be dancers,' I said. 'I don't.'

'What do you want then?' he asked, as I stood up.

One night he was waiting for me as I changed into my heavy outdoor clothes in order to go home in the early morning.

'I'll walk home with you,' he said, and put an arm under my elbow as we fell into step along streets that were slippery with ice. It was a winter night, November I think, with a little snow, and I shivered as the cold found a way under my clothes.

'Let us have a schnapps,' he urged. 'I know just the place. We can talk.'

He seemed to be well known in the cellar to which he led me. A young lady with hair piled high on her head looked me over with

20

disapproval as she came to take our order. 'Isn't she very young?' she asked.

'What will you drink?' asked Wilhelm.

I had little experience of alcohol and I suddenly craved the sweetness of that Palestine wine we sometimes drank on Jewish festivals.

'A sweet liqueur . . . yes. I will mix you a marvellous cocktail,' murmured Wilhelm.

The room was very hot and the contrast to the freezing street made me feel sleepy as Wilhelm helped me to take off my coat. The first sip of the cocktail he devised made me cough for all its sweetness, and had the effect of distancing me from everything else in the room. It seemed to me I was once again back home, required to perform for my father, and in that spirit I began to sing without being asked. One of the songs had been sung at the cabaret, a bitter song whose words I hardly understood.

The waitress who brought the drink he had devised for me stood listening till I finished and then said: 'She has a true voice. Be kind to her, Wilhelm.'

After that drink I can only remember fragments: being pulled and tugged up narrow stairs with the help of several people, as waves of sickness overcame me and soiled the floor, my clothes, and at last the bed to which I was helped and on which I lay ashamed and shaking. For a time I fell into a black sleep. Towards morning, Wilhelm got in beside me. I felt ugly and unclean from all the vomiting, and though I guessed he wanted to push his body into mine I kept my legs tightly closed together.

At length, irritated by resistance, he said, 'Prudish bitch! Can't you give anything?'

The reproach reached me in some dead, unhappy part of my brain, and I let him lower himself heavily on to my body, feeling nothing more than a little remote pain inside me as he did so, before we both fell asleep.

In the morning, I did not hate Wilhelm but myself. The memory I had of being sick and helpless filled me with loathing. In comparison with that public disgrace, the other event of the night seemed completely unimportant. I said nothing to Wilhelm as he took me back to my aunt. I think my main worry was that

21

someone from Westerborg's might have been in the café and witnessed my behaviour with such disgust that I would lose my job.

My aunt had not been up all night worrying about me, it soon appeared. She met me in a flurry of her own. I became aware of her anxiety even as I made my own wooden excuses.

'I was taken ill last night,' I explained.

Wilhelm backed me up. 'Something she ate. Temperature. Sickness. She still looks pale, doesn't she?'

My aunt looked over my white face, from which my eyes stared with more than usual intensity.

'You look dreadful,' she agreed. 'I'll phone Westerborg's . . . I just hope you don't have influenza.'

She seemed preoccupied, however, not to say agitated, and when Wilhelm had gone she began to explain her own troubles. M. Barbusse had returned much earlier than expected from Geneva, and found my things in the room he thought of as his study.

'He doesn't like families,' she said. 'Enough trouble with his own, that's why he comes here. I promised I'd talk to you.' She coughed as she lit a cigarette and tried to bring herself to ask me to find other lodgings. I knew what she was trying to say, but a kind of numbness prevented me helping her out. She put on a kettle and took my temperature (which was normal); made me a hot honey and lemon drink; but never once suggested putting me to bed. At length she found money from a drawer and pushed it into my hands.

'I'll find somewhere else,' I said. 'Don't worry.'

5

So once again I was displaced.

Wilhelm lived on Luzovstrasse in a dark top-floor room with one dim overhead bulb. In adjoining rooms, a terrier barked constantly and a Russian practised a sad violin all hours of the night. He lived mainly by black-market trading. He travelled into the countryside every week to barter with peasants, and spent the rest of the week in the city selling what he had found. For all he enjoyed making amorous arrangements from time to time for old comrades or school friends, he was not a pimp. At the corner of the big department store KDV you could see girls in high shiny boots and other equipment that signified their desire and ability to please. He liked to point them out to me, but he was far too cowardly to take on the role of protector in the streets of Berlin.

The nights I spent with Wilhelm were not likely to encourage any sensuality of my own, but in a curious way his heavy body at night, his grunts and even his groaning in his sleep made it easier for me to bear the strange world in which I now found myself. He had studied as a medical student for a time in Munich, but had been more interested in the Marxist revolution there than his studies. Whether he was present later on that freezing January night when thousands gathered on the Siegesallee, I didn't know, but he still spoke sadly of the Soviet Republic, and the murder of Rosa Luxembourg. I read with enthusiasm all the books he lent me.

These days I hardly saw my aunt. She was embarrassed at having had to look after herself at my expense. Once or twice she sent parcels of clothes and other gifts to me, and I was surprised one day to find a cardboard box that included the typewriter she had warned me against. A note inside soon explained the gesture. She thought I might like to sell it, she said. For herself, now that M. Barbusse was living with her on a regular basis, she had a superstitious horror of the thing.

Wilhelm looked at it with great interest. 'That will be useful,' he said at once. 'To the Party.'

I can't be sure which party exactly he had in mind, since he was a great joiner of parties.

'I can't use it,' I lied boldly.

The one sadness was that Wilhelm had no opinion of my talents, and positively disapproved of my reading and scribbling in the evenings.

'Listen, women aren't poets,' he explained to me. 'How many women poets can you name?'

I didn't know.

'Well then,' he said triumphantly.

As he was the only friend I had with a little education (I had none myself) it was Wilhelm to whom I showed my first scribbled songs.

'Women,' he would sigh. 'There's nothing to you. You're all shallow creatures.'

I had nothing to say to that, though I couldn't think what it meant. Did he mean I only had one layer of thought at a time? Did men have enormously more numerous layers? Were all women in this respect unlike their more fortunate brothers? I had read somewhere that women had no souls, and I was ready enough by then to believe I had no soul if Wilhelm told me so. A certain gloom filled me. I had begun to feel that if my songs were nothing, then I was nothing. Nothing, that is, except for those parts of my anatomy which Wilhelm worked urgently upon at night and from which I felt utterly remote.

I didn't like to believe my nature was so lacking in passion. The other girls thought of almost nothing but sex; they were always exchanging giggled confidences about their lovers' behaviour, and as I watched young bodies pushed up eagerly against one another in doorways I could see their experience was very different from mine. It was very disappointing.

One hot still evening in August, however, all that changed.

It was raining intermittently. Big splashes fell on the pinkish paving stones, then as soon as the rain stopped the colour of the stone dried from brown to pink again. It was my night off, and

Wilhelm was meeting an important client, so I was a customer for once at Westerborg's. There was a scuffle of applause, and Wilhelm said grumpily, 'We'd better sit down.'

As soon as we did, Wilhelm began to drink from a glass of brandy that had been left behind on the table from some earlier client, meanwhile holding my knee hard under the table.

'Don't drink so much,' I pleaded.

I was hungry and dipped some of the bread on the table into the mustard, a gesture he looked at with disgust. Presently a man with stubbly hair came out in front of the audience carrying a banjo. He had a cheap pair of glasses hanging loosely over his nose, a worker's cap and a jacket of shabby leather. He was little more than twenty. His thin body looked as if he had been undernourished for months, and his face looked defenceless, with a full underlip like a hurt child. Then he grinned at the audience and his grin, too, was childlike. I found myself watching with sudden intentness.

He sang with a harsh voice in a Swabian accent with heavy 'R' sounds. As he sang, the audience began to go quiet and listen; first to the story of a harlot going into the water after being ravished by a boatload of men, and then a ballad about a dead soldier stitched together and sent back into battle. Even Wilhelm's face was touched for a moment with some kind of interest.

'The war,' he said. 'It is all the war. Everything that is wrong with this country now is the war.'

When the song finished, I clapped involuntarily and without thought. We all did. I have heard a good deal of applause in my life now, and I know the quality of it. Some applause is polite, sustained; it is what is expected; it is decorous, even when bouquets are thrown. The applause that night was the sudden unexpected applause of sheer delight, as if the audience had been given a present of something they needed and did not otherwise know about.

The young man went back to a group of people, including a beautiful woman with short dark hair and an austere carriage who kissed him on his cheek.

'Stop staring,' said Wilhelm irritably.

'Who is he?' I asked impatiently.

25

'Everyone knows him,' said someone at the table in front of me.

'Well, I know him too,' said Wilhelm a little grudgingly. 'I knew him in my Munich days. He is some kind of poet.'

'But what is his name?'

There must have been a strange note in my voice, something a little unhinged, or perhaps sexually charged. Wilhelm frowned, with a curious unwillingness to help me. 'I have a business appointment,' he said, standing up and stretching.

'His name is Brecht,' said the man in front of me.

'That's it,' said Wilhelm, as if he needed the reminder.

6

I cannot remember now how I came to be walking along the seashore, with sand on my tongue, and a salty wind in my hair, but I know the Baltic sun was so bright that it made my eyes hurt. Probably a group of us had driven up to the coast together. There was certainly a car. And as I remember it there were many young men in striped bathing suits lying on the sand. My own swimsuit was suitably chaste, but it gave my rising figure an emphasis boldly inspected by Wilhelm's friends.

It was on that seashore I met Brecht again. He had a book under his arm as he fell into step beside me. 'I hear you are a Marxist?' he asked me seriously.

My new convictions were bookish enough, but I was flattered to have them known and agreed eagerly with the description.

'Tell me,' he murmured.

And so I expounded all I knew of labour and society and the world without property that awaited us, while he nodded at my side.

When I rejoined Wilhelm he looked sulky.

'What could you find to talk about with him?' he asked.

My explanation made him laugh. 'He doesn't need you to tell him all that,' he exclaimed patronizingly. 'A sixteen-year-old girl can have absolutely nothing to say on such matters. If you had, I would know.'

'Not necessarily,' I said, greatly daring. 'He seemed to encourage me, to bring out what there was in me.'

He frowned. 'He was flirting with you,' he said dismissively.

It was a new idea, and one I found instantly appealing.

A few days later I met Brecht again when he came to see Trude Westerborg, and recognized me casually. Wilhelm had not come to collect me and he asked if I needed to be walked home. I was too young, too healthy and too silly to have any fear of doing so, and in spite of his ruggedly proletarian clothes, I do not think he would have offered much protection. Nevertheless, I fell in eagerly with the suggestion.

We did not walk home directly, but along the Ku'damm, pausing to take a coffee. He enjoyed everything. As we sat, one of the pimps in the café was instructing a little whore just up from the country.

'Your handbag, Erika,' we heard him say. 'More jaunty.' And we laughed to hear the instruction.

'What do you read? I mean last night. In bed?' he asked me then.

'Poetry,' I confessed reluctantly. I should have preferred to have been able to mention a book about prize fighters, or some American gutter fiction.

'How old are you?' he muttered. 'Are you even sixteen?'

'Months ago,' I said.

He smiled at my firmness.

'Wilhelm told me you are writing a tragedy,' I said.

'No,' he said. 'I don't believe in it. I want to teach people not to be confused by their feelings.'

'Don't emotions always confuse?' I asked him.

He looked as if I had said something rather clever and I flushed with pleasure.

'I must have a drink of brandy,' he said then. 'They've pulled out my front tooth and smashed half my jaw.'

When he grinned I saw that several of his remaining teeth were brown with tobacco stains but for some reason that did not repel me.

'I write songs too,' I said timidly.

He had shrewd and sceptical eyes. 'The less people write the better,' he said. I opened my mouth to argue but he was laughing at me. 'Enjoy what you can do.'

'And it doesn't matter what?' I asked him.

'No,' he smiled, and stroked my arm.

We didn't go back to his room immediately. The sky was clouded, and there was a good deal of wind in the bushes as we took a short cut towards his flat. Groping through the foliage together, he gave

28

me a lot of kisses and squashed himself to me, but he seemed to want to talk more than anything else.

'What do you do?' I asked him.

'I smoke, gossip, mooch around,' he said. 'And read detective stories.'

'What about the girl you came to Westerborg's with?' I asked, greatly daring.

He seemed to have been thinking about her himself.

'She goes by car any time she likes,' he said after a pause. 'Has fur coats, rings, dresses, eats good food, likes music. What do you want to know?'

'Are you married to her?'

'She is having my child,' he said. 'She lives in Munich. Does it matter?'

It didn't matter to me.

'Maybe I'll sell my stuff soon,' he mused. 'A lot of people do.'

7

His apartment was a mess of papers and newspapers, and there was a faint sweetish smell mingled with a whiff of sour milk. I wondered why the squalor made me feel so much at home when my own home had always been so prissily clean. It was as if all the dirt and confusion related to some buried piece of myself.

'You need some help here,' I said, disguising my delight beneath a censorious air.

He smiled. 'Does it worry you?'

A copy of *Das Kapital* lay among his papers, but he hadn't read very far, I noticed. I was already looking at the poems, lying on the desk in marvellous disorder, and the words of his poetry flooded me.

'Perhaps I can help you put all this in order?'

At this he laughed. 'My dear child, I have a maid from Bavaria who would do that if I encouraged her, but I don't let her touch my papers.'

He was restlessly walking the room as he spoke. I wanted to know more about the play he was writing, but he shrugged my questions away. 'Do you know why people love tragedy? I'll tell you. It keeps their minds off being alone.'

'I hate to be alone,' I shuddered.

'I meant alone on this damned planet,' he said.

Then he put a hand on my breast and turned me towards him. I had taken no sexual pleasure in my life before that moment and I was unprepared for the extremity of desire, which was like a sickness as he opened my blouse and felt my breasts.

'Are you wet?' he asked me.

I didn't even know what he meant.

'Shall I see?' he asked. And he put his fingers between my legs, drawing them out and holding them under my nose so that I could for the first time smell my own sexual juices. I was astonished at their profusion and their odour. He insisted that I guide his hands, and I obeyed, trembling. The care and delicacy of his response was not something for which my experience with Wilhelm had prepared me. As his clever fingers rubbed the place I had found for him, he watched me with concern.

'You must take pleasure too,' he explained.

I never had. I didn't know I could. As he pressed himself into me I did, for the first time. Afterwards I was incoherent. I had become a woman and wanted him to know as much.

There was a huge tall tree, a silver birch, I think, with a trunk mottled in the way French painters show it, and dancing leaves that turned in the sunlight with a kind of dreamy glitter. That night as I looked out at it through the window from his bed I was happy. The tree made me happy. Or the world it represented. Sometimes the moon was very bright, and the tree very dark; and sometimes there was an owl hooting as if we were in the country. I asked him sleepily, 'Why do owls hoot? Doesn't it just alert their prey to their danger?'

But he was deeply asleep and did not attempt an answer.

I moved out from Wilhelm's room to one of my own, and saw Brecht two or three times a week. One evening he produced a sheaf of pencilled scribble diffidently. There was nothing domineering about him. He needed my help and I felt privileged to be able to do so.

'Can you type?' he asked.

Eagerly, I said that I could. Somewhere in my head my aunt's brazen and premonitory voice repeated a warning, but I did not listen. 'I have my own typewriter,' I said proudly. 'I can type in the mornings. I'll have it done in no time.'

He nodded as if he expected no less.

For one hot and wonderful month I typed his harsh words every morning, tasting their abrasive sweetness almost as if he were rubbing my most secret parts. And as a reward he took me to taverns in Berlin where it was possible to eat the Augsburg food he continued to prefer.

'Once anything is part of me,' he explained seriously, 'I like to keep hold of it for ever.'

31

I felt part of him then and saw nothing sinister in his wish. He preferred not to go out in the evenings. He worked on a big table under the window; anyone could come and read what he was doing. Sometimes he sat reading, but not as much as I did. He only read what he could use for his work. He liked people to come and see him, people who exchanged gossip, told stories and laughed. His hands directed the conversation, throwing a sharp question to one, answering another; always in charge.

'Chaplin,' some actor said. 'What is it you like so much about Chaplin?'

And he'd explain. 'He knows how to use farce. I like the way his face twitches.'

'What's wrong with the theatre we already have in Berlin?' somebody asked.

'It's no fun,' he said.

'You just mean you aren't accepted on it,' the voice jeered.

'You're right,' he snapped. 'Any more than the boxer Jack Dempsey could fight in a bar room. Someone would just knock him out with a chair.'

And we all laughed with him.

'A love story doesn't make a play, does it?' I said one evening. And that remark of mine amused him so much he subsided into his armchair shaking with silent laughter, so that his shoulders heaved, and I began laughing too.

'You said something like that last week,' someone pointed out.

'Yes, that's life,' he said.

I wasn't hurt by the laughter. On the contrary, when I saw him laugh I knew the world was an amusing and bearable place. I learnt from him all the time. When he sang, I listened carefully to the way he cut his words as if with a guillotine. The way every word was separate and clear as a pebble.

It was the only training I had.

Sometimes when he was restless we walked about Berlin together; he liked the streets of the city, though I knew he missed the fields and lakes of his Bavarian landscape. The best of it was the talking. There was so much I had to learn from him. He told me about Wedekind, whom he had seen lecture, and the Blaue Reiter, and the Neue Sachlichkeit Art, and took me to galleries because looking at paintings was free.

I don't know how he earned his money; he was always angling for contracts; and his clothes were always shabby; but he managed to find money for brandy and cigars. And sometimes we went to Schlichters in Lutherstrasse, which had a good cold buffet with salads.

One evening I arrived late at his rooms to find him moodily playing the guitar. He had taken off his spectacles and his face looked defenceless and sad.

'Everything I've been writing lately has been bad and ordinary,' he said. 'If only I could only calm down and enjoy simple things . . . the eating of potatoes, for instance.'

I laughed and came and sat next to him as closely as I could, but he stroked my leg in a preoccupied manner. Something seemed to be on his mind.

'People are nastier than you imagine,' he said. 'Do they fondle you much? At Westerborg's?'

I was immensely flattered by what I took to be jealousy, and I hastened to reassure him. 'No,' I said. 'I don't let them.'

He patted my hand.

I don't know what powers of intuition led him to say as much, but something *had* certainly happened which might have given him cause for jealousy. The only other passion of my life had been awoken that very morning when I had my first opportunity to sing to Trude Westerborg, and she had given me a week's trial. The experience had been intoxicating. I discovered I could make electricians turn round to look at me when I sang. And waitresses, who had hitherto despised me, come up to add their congratulations. In a word I had discovered I was a natural performer.

And when I sang to that half-empty café for Trude I discovered something else as I saw heads turn, eyes darken and strangers attend. When I sang I was loved. And I was no longer alone. The girls who had shared my days as a waitress clustered round me with strange expressions.

'When did you learn to do that?'

'You won't be doing the dishes any more.'

A man who had watched me with burning eyes, came up to me and said, 'What are you doing, I must see you this evening,' but I

33

had learnt how to keep men at bay with a glare. He fell back in front of my savage eyes, his sexuality subdued.

Some instinct kept me from telling Brecht about my good fortune.

The satisfaction I drew from receiving my first pay from the cabaret was almost sexual. I opened the brown envelope slowly, and fingered the notes within. They were huge notes, of course; two million, I think, was the face value. It would not buy more than a week's living in those days, but I took out the notes reverently.

To my mind came the image of that first girl I had seen in the Munich café, drawing money from her red garter, and pressing it into Wilhelm's hand with a bold gesture. I knew now that her earnings were from prostitution, but I still had the same flicker of pleasure in the memory. I had a poignant sexuality on stage that had something to do with that erotic experience. The audience knew the passion I felt for them, and gave me back what I asked.

Somehow I said none of this to Brecht. I felt it would bring a frown to his face, that it would make him insecure, that he might even resent this new piece of my life. And I wasn't deceiving myself. When the success of my first night was so ecstatic that I immediately had an offer to play in a Strauss operetta, and another piece on the Ku'damm, I could suppress my news no longer and I saw exactly what I had feared in his eyes.

'I'll never move away from you,' I said in a rush. 'Never. I promise.'

He patted my buttocks thoughtfully.

It surprised me that Brecht should want my fidelity, and I was enormously pleased by the evidence of such interest, which I took to represent the seriousness of our relationship. I don't know how long it was before I realized that the fidelity that Brecht exacted from me was not something he was offering himself.

I knew he was married. It seemed to have nothing to do with us. Nothing to do with Berlin. I had seen her, of course. Marianne Zoft. An opera singer. A provincial opera singer I reminded myself. She had Brecht's child. And there was another child somewhere from an earlier girlfriend. But I didn't think of them.

34

They had nothing to do with his warm body in mine, or his fingers between my legs.

'You are so good,' he said to me as his hands fondled and stroked my body. 'So innocent.'

And I purred at the praise. He made me feel good, kind and happy. He made it possible for me to love myself.

Once, when we looked in the mirror, the narrowness of our two faces and something about the droop of our mouths, made me say 'How alike we look.'

Then he grinned and the physical resemblance was lost.

I have often thought about that likeness. It was not the likeness of brother and sister, but Narcissus and the mirror image, or rather the perfected image in the pool. When I tried to speak of that, he shrugged it away.

When I looked in the mirror I saw everything I had once disliked in my face but I no longer heard the voices of my childhood complaining about my black eyes and my sallow skin. Instead, I looked and felt beautiful.

Brecht worked when he wanted to. He gave me sheets to type and I tapped away happily. It didn't worry him that I was there, and sometimes I scribbled alongside him. One night, he came over to see what I was doing.

'I have written a ballad,' I said hesitantly.

He read what I had done. 'You imitate me,' he pointed out.

I knew as much.

'Sing it,' he asked.

It was the first time Brecht had listened to me sing. I had stolen a folk tune but the words were mine and I had written of two children asleep under a coat in the doorway of a butcher's shop, holding one another tight to keep warm. I knew my voice came out as harshly as a singer of a Moritat ballad as I described the temptation in the eyes of the butcher who had no meat for his shop.

When I had finished, Brecht stood up and looked at me with a new intentness. 'We could work on that,' he said seriously.

That night we stood together looking out at the wet trees. The sky had cleared after a rain storm and the moonlight caught the edges of the leaves, giving the whole street an eerie beauty. For

35

the first time in a long while it was possible to see the stars which were high above us like points of light.

'You see that constellation?' he asked me.

I stared up hopefully. I remembered a few school lessons about the skies, and it seemed fitting that he should instruct me in the heavenly bodies, since I had only been happy from the moment we met.

'It is Orion,' he said. 'Remember. It is our world. Wherever we are we can look up at the sky and remember one another.'

It was as if he had made a present of the stars to me.

'I love you,' I said.

'Come.' He led me away from the window. 'My little singer.' And we made love with all the joy that we knew how to bring each other, and without any thought of anything outside the room we occupied.

That October I remember the first uneasy panic because my period was late. The leaves on the trees were a translucent yellow, and the sunshine so brilliant that I was dazzled when walking along the streets to buy vegetables. But my happiness was overlaid with terror. Brecht received the news moodily, and unhelpfully.

'I must get rid of it, of course,' I said.

I was unprepared for his fury.

'You won't,' he said. 'I won't let you.'

It was as if he felt the little foetus were himself, as if I were threatening to murder him. As if, in threatening to unseat that little globe of possible life, I made him feel insecure about trusting me.

Perhaps fortunately, the choice wasn't left to me. One night on a bus I felt the first dark blood beginning between my legs. At first I was simply relieved, but then as it spread in a flood down my stockings, I was frightened. I remember clearly that my fear was nothing to do with any danger to myself. As the blood began to drip on the floor I was afraid that what was happening would be visible to any curious passenger. And I was filled with shame. Like a relic of my childhood. At a moment when my one and only life might have been in danger, I thought of myself as dirty. The blood that was leaking from me, leaving me white and faint, seemed a sign of pollution. I jumped off the bus, and tried to run along the street to escape that shame, horrified to see I was leaving a trail of blood as I did so. The seat of my new coat was wet at the back. All I could think of was that people would see the blood as I ran.

When at length I reached my room, my knickers, stockings and skirt were bright red and dripping. I flung them in a bucket, and lay on the bed. I knew I needed a doctor, but I fainted before doing anything about it, and was still lying across my bed when my landlady found me.

I was young. I survived. That part of me which felt my own female self like a stain returned briefly, but my problem was for the moment over. Brecht was suspicious I had done something to procure the abortion, but I persuaded him otherwise.

About this time, Brecht discovered I was Jewish. In those days he had the usual casual anti-Semitism of his class, which did not trouble me. It was in the air as an issue: the Jews were said to have been responsible for Germany's defeat. He wanted to know how I felt about it. I had hardly given it a thought.

'Your race has been abused for so long, over so many centuries,' he mused. 'Never wiped out for all the Christian hatred. You must be very tough.'

'Women might say the same,' I said, a little sullenly. For I had begun to link the two parts of myself.

I went on living where I was. He now preferred to come to my room so he could choose when to do so. As a result I went home every night after work directly in case he should either be there, or about to arrive. He liked that particularly since it meant he was now more or less the only man I saw. I annoyed him once by praising another writer I met and it upset him. Brecht was not yet well known in Berlin, even if he had been given the Kleist prize and his poems were coming out very soon from a famous imprint. He particularly hated Thomas Mann.

'Don't you see? He makes us feel the middle classes are decent,' he said. 'And that's why he's dangerous.'

I drank in every word.

8

With the money I was earning, I could afford to go to the theatre more often. I saw Picator's wonderful spotlit productions with relish. Was it then I heard Josephine Baker? We all loved black jazz.

One evening Brecht and I were sitting in Schlichters restaurant when I became aware of a dark, good-looking woman sitting at the next table. Brecht had his back to her, but I could see she was trying to catch his attention, and after a time he became aware of her eagerness and turned his head.

They exchanged smiles.

As I saw the sweetness in his face as he smiled, a shaft of jealousy went through me. In that moment I knew they were lovers, recent lovers; that they had touched one another intimately. Her eagerness was so clear. She could not join us at the table quickly enough.

A little darkness entered my soul as I tried to persuade myself I was mistaken.

'Elizabeth Hauptmann,' Brecht said quickly. 'She translates from the English. She is going to work for me as my secretary.' And once again they exchanged that warm smile of complicity. She did not look as if she had any more money than I did; her coat was shabby and darned at the pockets. But she wore her hat aslant her face with an elegance I thought of as American, and she had good shoes and stockings.

'I see,' I said.

She was about ten years older than I was, with neat features. And she was going to type for him, instead of me.

'What do you think of this?'

Brecht passed me some typescript and I swallowed. It was difficult to read by the dim lighting, and I said so. He was disappointed in my reaction, and indeed I was furious with myself as he stood up.

38

'I have a meeting with the director of the Schiff,' he said.

We were left together, his new friend and I. Her eyes dropped before mine.

That night I lay under his sheet and waited for him to come to bed. He was working with absorption at his table. I was angry with him and wanted to express my anger at the injustice of what was happening. I wanted him to know how unhappy he had made me. I had no intention of blaming him but I wanted him to repent and ask for forgiveness, murmur to me that I was good and pure, and that we shared a particular constellation of stars. I lay waiting for a long time, while he gave no sign of coming to bed. At length I had to prop myself up on my elbow and speak to him. He peered at me over his glasses, not so much unrepentant as unaware that I was angry. A part of me wanted nothing more than to have him cross the room and get into bed at my side. The thought of his comforting body next to mine was something I longed for so much that only a separate black and forsaken need made me say, 'Have you slept with her? Bess Hauptmann?'

I would have liked him to deny it. Or fall at my knees and beg for my absolution. Instead, he said calmly, 'Once or twice.'

He was totally unashamed.

'When?' I croaked miserably.

He looked up then shrewdly, his black eyes twinkling with knowing malice. 'How does it matter to you what I do when I'm not with you?' he asked.

He came over at this point and put his warm familiar hand on me, so that my body responded with an aching recognition. 'Women have to put up with these things,' he said.

He was perfectly calm and I believed him. If he said so, then this was how life was. It couldn't be anything else.

'I've taken two of your songs for the new play,' he said casually. Without him, I thought, I amount to nothing. I am of value only because he loves me.

9

The singing work I had was intermittent but sufficient. One day I was singing in a small and not particularly salubrious café near the Ku'damm when I recognized a familiar, heavily built man at a table close to the cabaret floor. It was my father.

I watched him from the darkness. He seemed in sombre mood. Sitting with him was a young but weary-faced girl dressed like a cheap whore in the style of the times. My heart banged underneath my ribs as I watched. My mouth was dry with fear. And the girl's attention wandered round the other tables. He did not seem much concerned with her. A bottle of Marc stood on the table, and once or twice he lifted it and drank from the mouth.

When the time came for me to perform I had a moment of panic, though as I walked out into the lights my pulse steadied. The music for one of my harshest songs began but I had lost my usual sense of the audience and saw instead only the silent figure of my father staring at his table. As I tried to fight off that paralysing awareness, I heard a treacherous and unmistakable rustling at the edges of the room. I was losing the attention of the crowd. My power was failing. Someone began to cough. On an impulse I walked over to the piano and changed the order of my programme. Since I could feel only tenderness at that moment, I realized there was no sense in trying to put any other emotion into my voice. I began to sing one of the sentimental songs from my childhood, which I usually introduced as an ironic balance to the rest, but I sang now with pure sweet tones. The audience stilled again.

As I sang, he lifted his head and turned hazily towards me. A little spite touched me as I saw him peering with half recognition. I would have liked to bring tears to his eyes with the thought of a daughter lost. I felt so moved myself, bowing to the applause, that my throat hurt me.

As soon as I had finished singing, I went over to my father's table. The girl he was with looked up at me with startled eyes, so I suppose my advance seemed alarming. My father turned blank eyes on me.

'Frieda?' he asked uncertainly.

I looked down boldly. 'The same.'

If he had taken my hand or showed any tenderness, I should have flung myself into his arms. But instead he stared at me. 'So that's what you're doing, you whore. Exhibiting your body to strangers.'

His voice was thick with drink.

I looked at the young girl at his side with some irony. She stood up, collecting her small bag hastily.

'Your mother is ill,' said my father heavily.

I bit my lip. I had not once thought of her in all my confused emotions at seeing him again.

'The streets,' he said. 'A daughter on the streets. The shame will kill me.'

He made such a pious face to accompany these sentiments that I think I may have laughed. His manner changed then, and he bent forward towards me, his eyes sharpening with anger. 'Don't lay it at my door, you bitch. It was in your nature, your own wicked nature. You are a creature of the gutter. Don't purse your lips at me, it was your own foul thoughts, your own wishes, your own foul stink . . .' He grabbed at my haunches as he spoke, and his fingers gripped me painfully, as if to point up the viciousness of his remarks. 'You can smell your own urine, your own excrement.'

I flinched at the brutality.

'To tell your mother what you did . . . Do you expect me to forgive you? Monster . . .'

There were stinging tears in my eyes.

Luckily, at that moment his girl companion returned and held out her hand with a cheeky gesture.

'You still have my cloakroom ticket, Poppa,' she said, while her whole demeanour hinted that she needed some other payment for her company that evening.

'Here,' I said, while my father fumbled in his pocket. She grasped the paper notes I gave her.

41

When she had gone, I asked him more composedly, even with some amusement in my voice, 'And who is she?'

He stared at me morosely, impressed perhaps by the casual gift of money and something hard in my gaze.

He did not reply, and I went on sitting at the table, still uncertain of how to treat him. I still longed for him to behave differently towards me. I had never been in more need of tenderness. The only man I had ever found to love had betrayed me with another woman. And here was my father, who could have comforted and helped me. I wanted to beg him for kindness. Even now, the wide shoulders suggested protection to me.

'Damn you,' he said. 'Don't you worry your mother with it, do you hear? She has enough to bother about.'

After a moment's puzzlement, I realized that he was afraid I would tell my mother that he had been carousing with a prostitute. He had no sense of my need, nor any interest in satisfying it. There was no love or tenderness in him for me. Realizing as much, I stood up and rushed away from him blindly.

As I was leaving the café I recognized Lotte Lenya. She was looking her stunning best, her lips a brilliant red, her eyes flashing. She caught my hand and her eyes searched my face. 'I've got a job for you,' she said.

Probably nothing else that anyone could have said to me would have halted my headlong flight. Afterwards I guessed that she knew everything about me and that her own experience was not so different from mine.

'Come and see me tomorrow and I'll tell you about it.'

PART TWO

THE THREEPENNY OPERA

'You've got no 'eart, Johnnie
You're no damn good, Johnnie
You've gone away, Johnnie
Without a line.
I'm still in love, Johnnie
Like at the start, Johnnie . . .
Take that pipe out of your mouth, you swine.'

Brecht: 'Surabaya Johnnie'

1

Lotte Lenya and I played in some of the same shows, often in small parts. Her radiant friendliness and her oddly irregular face made me smile. One day she came up to me and said, 'You have a real talent, little one. But you should learn to dance.' And she arranged for me to go to a friend of hers for dancing lessons, knowing I was out of work for a week.

It must have been some time in 1927 when I grew close to Lotte. I always admired her, but she made me timid; and I could not understand what she could see in me. She was working as an understudy for Juliet in a theatre near Alexanderplatz, which gave her a great deal of free time, and she was planning to perform some of Kurt Weill's songs at a summer festival in Baden Baden.

I cannot have seemed a rival. I was still gawky, with an uncertain dress sense, sometimes falling in with my aunt's flamboyant preferences and sometimes dressing in whatever lay to hand. Lenya exuded raw sexuality without any of the attributes of natural beauty. Her body was fit and slender but there was nothing voluptuous in her shape; it was the way she knew how to stand that suggested sexual pleasure. She had full thick lips, often painted a harsh red, and her grin showed large teeth set widely apart. The two sides of her face did not entirely match. It was sheer naked libidinous energy that made her attractive.

And for some reason Lenya took on the role of my mentor. Stronger and more worldly women have often protected me. She was the first of them, unless you count my brave and fluttery Aunt Clara.

'Like this,' she would say to me laughing, belting my coat and turning up the collar at the back of my neck. 'There. Why don't you get one of those big soft hats? You could pull it down over your forehead like I do, and people would bend to look into your mysterious brown eyes.'

45

In those days almost half the work I had came through her; I did everything she said. Or most things. I could not emulate her casual promiscuity.

'Of course I love Kurt,' she would say to me. 'What has that got to do with it?'

The first time I saw her in her own setting, Kurt was in another room playing the piano. They lived in an apartment in Luisen-platz. There were huge dark paintings of hunting dogs on the walls and black furniture. I found it very impressive. She called through to Kurt to say I was here but he made no response and she found that amusing.

'I might as well not be in the house,' she said, and came and sat very close to me on the black couch. She helped me take off my coat, and then surveyed my narrow, girlish body speculatively. 'Why are you so faithful?' she asked with a throaty catch in her voice that was new to me. After a moment she put a hand on my knee. I was a little frightened, but a shiver of the interest Brecht aroused went through me. She saw as much and smiled.

'You must have more fun. Living so virtuously is bad for you.'

'I don't feel virtuous,' I said.

'Of course you don't. You feel sinful. That is the trouble with you. And yet you have such talent.' She sighed.

'What kind of talent do you mean?' I asked, greedy for a little praise.

She jumped up laughing. 'You know very well you have a wonderful voice. And the words of your songs are brilliant. Weill is going to set one of your verses.'

This was news to me and my eyes went round with pleasure.

'First we are going to Baden Baden,' she said. 'We are performing *Mahagonny*.'

I knew about that. Bess Hauptmann had written the first draft of the songs and Brecht had made them over.

'Maybe you can be one of the girls in the brothel,' said Lenya, drawing her hand down my leg, and laughing. 'Let me see. Put your leg up. Not like that. Better. The skirt has to fall so we can see the curve of your thigh. What do you think?'

I wasn't sure whether Brecht would let me act in his new play and said so.

46

'He is very hard on you,' she said, frowning.

'Do you like to work with him?' I asked timidly.

She nodded, smiling good-naturedly. 'I learn a lot from him. He teaches me how to forget the audience,' she explained. 'To be myself. With ordinary human feelings. I have such terrible stage fright.'

It was another paradox about her.

At that moment Weill came into the room, blinking a little, like an animal who has been underground. He was neatly dressed, a short, balding man with round dark-rimmed glasses; and that afternoon he seemed preoccupied.

Brecht did not want me to come to Baden Baden. I accepted his decision; I had no choice. He was busy now every evening; talking to the stage designer about his plan to set the Songspiel in a boxing ring; he wanted Lenya to appear nude, I remember, but the festival management objected. Kurt, too, I supposed. I once asked Lenya whether she and Brecht had had an affair, and she laughed.

'No, little one. We are too alike. We leave each other well alone.'

Did I force Brecht to choose between Bess Hauptmann and myself? Matters were not so simple as one might imagine. She took over most of the secretarial work almost at once; she was far more competent than I was, and spoke several other languages. Brecht did not try to conceal they were also lovers, but just *because* there was no deception I did not see how to express my resentment. I even continued to turn to him for emotional support.

For instance, I told him about my father's unkindness.

'*Fathers*,' he said. 'What do you expect? Ordinary bourgeois life is full of such cruelty. Don't try and set it up.'

I said I wanted love and warmth, if that was what he meant. 'I want to be the woman that matters to you,' I said.

'As you do,' he assured me.

'I don't want to share you,' I said.

The dark eyes behind his spectacles went black and still. Then he smiled and left.

47

About eleven one night, when he had said he would visit me, I formed a doomed certainty that he was in Bess Hauptmann's bed. I was too agitated to wait and see. Instead I put on my coat. Who knew where she lived? Lenya, I decided.

She answered my telephone call with a throaty, sleepy voice. She gave me the address.

'I hope you are being sensible,' she said.

Probably she guessed I was not. In matters of sexuality Lenya guessed everything and she probably could hear my driven, hopeless state.

With the address on a piece of paper, I took a taxi to the street where Bess Hauptmann lived. It was a poor enough neighbourhood, with few cars of any kind. The shop fronts were broken and boarded up. The streets were very silent. Outside the address Lenya had given me sat Brecht's new Steyr car. It was unmistakable. I paid the taxi and got out and stood in the road. I must have looked exceedingly odd because the cab driver called out through his windows towards me.

'Are you all right, Miss?'

I was not all right.

I crossed the road. On the wall of the apartmenthaus there were bells, and I saw one labelled 'Hauptmann'. I rang it savagely. Nothing happened. I rang it again. And again. I don't know what I hoped to achieve. Presently to my surprise a sleepy-looking Hauptmann appeared in a thick, woollen dressing gown; her pale, scrubbed cleanliness angered me. I pushed past her.

She had left open the door to her flat and I entered without any exchange of courtesies. In the living room within, poorly lit, stood a table with a typewriter and many manuscripts scattered over it. Fully dressed and poring through the papers on the table, stood Brecht. He turned with an interrogative expression as I came in.

'If you don't mind,' said Bess Hauptmann coolly, 'I think I'll go back to bed.'

And that is what she did, leaving Brecht to go on looking through the papers.

I was nonplussed.

He didn't ask what I was doing there, or how I had found him.

In desperation I began to look around the room to see what books she read, this English-seeming lady. She read Kipling and Villon, I saw. And there were copies too of Jack London and Ring Lardner. I looked back at Brecht and saw he was following my progress round the room with an amused expression.

'You have a curious spirit,' he said. 'Like me.'

A great weariness overcame me. 'Come home,' I urged him.

'I've not finished,' he said.

'If you don't come now –' I said in a threatening tone, and stopped. He looked up at me with great surprise. 'That is the end, then,' I said, with a flash of conviction and anger. And as I said so a momentary strength filled me.

He stood there sadly.

I wanted to scream, 'Persuade me, you fool. Explain to me. Say anything to make me change my mind.'

But instead he said, to my horror, 'If that's what you want.'

'I think so,' I said, with craven uncertainty.

'Can you get home?'

It occurred to me there would be no taxis, but I was too miserable to be afraid. 'I'll walk,' I said.

For a moment I thought he might offer to take me in his car, knowing the dangers of the streets in Berlin at night that year, but he nodded and even smiled.

'It isn't far,' he agreed.

I cannot remember how I found my way home, or whether anyone called after me, or tried to help me. I saw nothing, and felt a kind of blankness only eased by the taste of the rain on my lips. Probably it was heavier rain than I thought, because I arrived back at my own room with my hair streaming wetly. I sat and towelled it with only one thought on my mind. It was over.

And then the real loneliness began, for which the pains of jealousy had been an inadequate preparation. To whom did I matter? Who cared what became of me? The certainty of the world's indifference paralysed me like a South American poison.

Waking the next day, I could not move from the bed. The blackness overcame me. It was impossible to eat. Was I dying? I certainly felt as if I no longer had any existence of my own. Who was I, if I was no longer Brecht's girl?

The day went by in a terrible stasis of grief, and by nightfall the pain was so intense I opened a bottle of gin and sat looking at the world through the dull green glass until I had reduced the pain to a manageable loss. I think I sat there crooning, helplessly drunk, until at last I was glad to fall into my bed with head pounding in the early hours of the morning.

Unfortunately, as the first morning light came into the room the pain was back again. At first it was just an unnamed hurt; I knew it as something I had to wake into. Then, waking, the emptiness filled me.

I had broken with Brecht.

I was alone.

The next few nights I found it impossible to drop off to sleep because I was too cowardly to face that waking knowledge. I can't remember who it was lent me the white tablets which brought relief to my snapping nerves.

At any rate, waking up refreshed after that first real sleep in a week, I had a sudden treacherous optimistic memory: Brecht might not have realized that I intended to finish our relationship altogether. I thought back to what I had said, to see if it seemed irreversible. In my memory this was far from the case. Moreover, I recalled that the song he had wanted to use in the new play had never been put in his hands. I had, therefore, an excuse to go round to the theatre and hand it to him.

At the thought of being able to see Brecht again, even if only to exchange a few friendly words with him, I was flooded with a new sensation, which I gradually recognized as relief. If, in some buried part of myself, I knew that seeing him would cure nothing, even if I understood nothing had changed, the mere possibility of seeing him restored me.

I rose from my bed and found it was now possible not only to make a cup of coffee, but to eat some bread and honey. I pondered on the lesson of this. Clearly, I thought, what is so necessary to my physiology cannot be given up.

I knew where he would be. He was rehearsing. The only thing

that worried me was that the rehearsal might not be in the rooms used the week before. I am not sure what play they were working on. I have in my mind something raunchy and violent, and the rooms I see brightly lit before my eyes are bare-boarded, with a white half-curtain, and I know the door I opened into them led from an unmistakably Berlin street. At any rate, I knew where the rehearsals were going on, and I hurried towards them. The only anxiety I had as I pushed past startled people in my eagerness was that he might not be there. Once inside the square, harshly lit room I became conscious of a great echoing voice, and saw Bess Hauptmann eating a sandwich, perched on a chair and taking notes. And there was Brecht, unshaven and scruffy, marching up and down explaining something.

As soon as I saw him, I felt as calm and happy as if I had been given a drug. Everything became very clear. I could no more give him up than oxygen. He saw me approaching, and smiled, and immediately it was as if nothing had ever been wrong.

2

Why did I put up with this relationship? My aunt asked the same question.

'What is so special about *him*?' she asked.

I tried to explain my attempt to break away and how ill it had made me.

She shook her head. 'Everyone says he's going to do something marvellous, but he's not done anything much yet,' she said. 'Has he?'

I decided she meant something which made him a great deal of money and that she hardly acknowledged success in any other terms. In this, she retained a sense of the world learnt in the bourgeois comfort of my father's house long ago. It didn't seem worth engaging in battle over it. In any case, Brecht had a lively sense of the same values.

'He's a great poet,' I said.

'Is he?' said my aunt grimly. 'Who says so?'

'Everyone. And he won the Kleist prize,' I remembered.

'What is he trying to do in the theatre?' demanded my aunt. 'People don't want plays that saw at one's nerves.'

'Well –' I began.

I had seen him sitting in front of unfinished work, and I knew he had to keep such doubts to himself. My aunt, however, was off on the track of her own muttering thoughts about my rival, Bess Hauptmann.

'She's some kind of secretary, isn't she?' she asked.

'She's a bit more than that,' I admitted reluctantly.

'What is she like?' asked my aunt, with the eagerness of an experienced campaigner planning to outflank an enemy.

I told her what I knew. 'Her mother is American,' I said. 'Brecht likes that. He likes everything American: detectives, gangsters, Charlie Chaplin . . .' America, I remembered, was the place Brecht wanted to explore once he was rich and famous. We were going to drive through the prairies together and enjoy the fleshpots in the wicked cities of the plain.

'Who is her father?' asked my aunt.

'German. A country doctor. Used to serving the old aristocracy,' I said in a rush. 'Very grand. Doesn't approve of Bess trying to be a writer.'

'So that's what she's trying to be,' nodded my aunt.

'She translates,' I said. But I knew she was more than a translator.

'How does she live?' asked my aunt.

I explained that she kept herself by doing whatever tutorial or translating work came along, and my aunt lifted her equine nose into a sniff. 'Dear me,' she said, as if puzzled. 'Does she help him in some way?'

My aunt had a witchy prescience, and she had put her finger on something important. Bess Hauptmann's talents were ideally suited to Brecht's present needs, and I knew as much, though I tried to stress other matters. 'She's very beautiful. Soft brown hair. Speaks gently. Wonderfully dressed,' I went on.

'Hm,' said my aunt, displeased. 'Is she now?' She pulled all her optimism together nevertheless, for my sake. 'Then they must make an odd couple.'

About this time I had a small part in a play. There was no music. I had only two lines to say as a maid. The whole would have had no importance if it had not given me my first chance to meet the great actress Helene Weigel.

It was a shabby theatre, I remember. The dressing room stank of stale powder and smoking oil from kerosene stoves. After the show, I sat in front of a mirror which needed silvering and watched Weigel taking off her greasepaint. She looked tired and pale; her face was rather plain without make-up. Offstage she was silent, almost morose. Timidly, I congratulated her on her performance. She nodded, pleasantly enough but without smiling. 'The play was nothing,' she said.

Presently I recognized the actor Alexander Granach coming towards her; I had heard they were lovers, and I was rather impressed by that. He was so handsome and well dressed; his success suited him. He approached Weigel and smiled in the mirror. She smiled back without any particular animation in her face. He may have suggested that they go and eat at Schlichters. She shook her head. At any rate he seemed to feel her refusal as a rebuff. My attention was only caught when they began talking about Brecht.

'What do women see in him?' Granach was saying. 'He's as thin as a priest and he dresses like a truck driver.'

I can't remember exactly what Weigel replied, but it was clear that she was amused by Granach's description, and that Granach was viciously jealous.

'He's never even had a show in Berlin,' he said, almost reproachfully.

'There are things he can teach me,' Weigel said, altogether indifferent to soothing him. I had never heard such confidence in a woman's voice. She seemed to know nothing of my connection with Brecht, and when she caught my eyes, which had begun to fix themselves on her, she smiled without anxiety.

For the first time I realized that she had some arrangement to meet Brecht that evening, and I surveyed her narrowly. What I saw was reassuring. She was a handsome woman, but there was something too strong in her face for feminine charm, and I could not feel her as a threat in the struggle for Brecht's affections.

The following day Brecht came in to see me to collect a couple of songs he had promised to make over for me, and I asked about Weigel.

'A wonderful actress,' I began. 'Isn't she?'

'The best in Berlin,' he agreed at once. 'And a wonderful woman.'

'How do you mean that?' I asked carefully.

'She cooks Augsburg food,' he explained. 'As finely as the cook in my mother's house used to make it. And apple strudels. Better than Vienna.'

'How does she have time?' I asked, a little petulantly.

'Oh, she has a maid,' he said. 'Her parents help her. They are wealthy Viennese Jews.'

I was surprised, because I had always thought Jewish daughters were not supposed to go on the stage. 'Do they approve then?'

He laughed at the idea. 'They help anyway.'

And then he came over to me and lifted my skirt above my knickers without any preliminary gestures. Rather to my own disgust, I was instantly excited, and when he eased my knickers down I was ready to lie on the carpet. Instead he pressed himself into me as we stood, and I experienced only a remote echo of the pleasure I usually enjoyed.

When he pulled my dress down I said, a little snappily, 'That was quick.'

'Well,' he said, 'I'm in a hurry. I have to move my flat.'

'Why? What is happening?' I asked, my irritation immediately dispersing.

I can't remember whether he was still directing *Edward II* in Munich, but he diverted my question and began to talk about actors who didn't know their craft.

'Most of them wouldn't eat if they had to understand their lines,' he said.

I agreed with him, and after he had gone wondered why he had never explained why or where he was moving. But I knew why I had not pressed him further. I was afraid.

A few weeks later I heard rumours that Weigel was pregnant. I was sitting in Schlichters, and the woman who said as much gave me a sly look at me which I didn't at first understand. Then she said crudely, 'Brecht is the father. Everyone knows.'

I didn't believe her and put my tongue out. Afterwards, when Brecht did not turn up to eat as we had arranged, I went home. I guessed he was working with Bess. She had translated part of an eighteenth-century English play, John Gay's *Beggar's Opera*, and Brecht had been very excited with the thought of turning the story into something modern. I don't remember whether he had yet sold the idea to the director of the Schiffbauerdamm Theatre, but there was some talk of the next season opening with it.

These days I phoned Bess's flat without embarrassment. Her voice when she answered was oddly alert, I thought, and when I asked for Brecht there was no mistaking the stress in her reply. 'So, he isn't with you?'

'No,' I said. 'I hope he is all right.'

This was not as disingenuous as it sounded. Only a week earlier a friend of ours who had been involved in an agitprop play which Brecht had written had been set upon in the streets and thrown through a plate-glass window. His injuries had been extensive, and so far no one had been charged with the assault.

'I hope he won't be picked on,' I found myself saying nervously. 'The Nationalists say he is decadent.'

'Don't worry,' she said harshly. 'He'll be tucked up comfortably by now.'

Emboldened by so much interchange, I suddenly found myself confiding in her the rumour that had been circulating over the dinner table,

'I expect it's true,' she said rather wearily, but without particular anxiety. From this I deduced that she had little sense of Weigel as a sexual rival. 'She cooks for him like his mother,' she said. 'And she's lending him her Spigernstrasse flat.'

It was the first I had heard of this, and after the first shock I knew it must be so.

'Do you think that is where he is?' I asked.

'No,' she said, and now the flicker of something like fear in her voice was unmistakable. 'There must be someone else.'

When I put down the telephone, I had begun to consider Bess as an ally rather than an enemy.

I still did about half Brecht's typing. Piles of his scribbled notes were brought round, not always by Brecht himself, always with great urgency; I never refused to do what he asked. In between cabaret performances, or on days when other girls went to the country or lay around enjoying a lazy time, I typed for him. Neatly, carefully, unresentfully, I typed for his publishers, I typed for his actors, I typed anything and everything he asked me to type without asking for money and without complaint. I had time. I lived quietly in those days.

There was a kind of daily violence in the streets that frightened me far more than the speeches of politicians, but I think I had not connected the two closely until my Aunt Clara turned up one night on my doorstep with her face streaming blood. I was astonished to see her, and brought her in with my heart banging, while she fussed about the damage that had been done to the feathers of her new boa and seemed unaware of the blood that continued to pour from a gash in her forehead.

'It needs stitching,' I said grimly.

At that her face blanched. She refused to consider going to a hospital. 'Get me a drink,' she said. 'I'll be all right. I've got good healing skin.'

I brought her a glass of whisky which she gulped down, her hands shaking.

'What happened?' I asked her.

'This filthy neighbourhood,' she frowned.

I filled her glass again.

'I wouldn't be here if Barbusse were still in Berlin. I was walking along the Ku'damm, minding my own business, when I saw a crowd of brownshirts, wearing their swastikas – boys really, no more – so I just went on walking and one of them shouted out.'

I looked at my aunt's bold, handsome face with its red lips and black hair and saw how badly she had been frightened.

'I tried to get away from them, but one of them caught my arms. You know what they shouted, don't you, Frieda?'

She shuddered when I shook my head.

'Jewish whore,' she whispered. 'Jewish whore.'

I felt terror more than sympathy and could only repeat her words feebly.

'Look at my face,' she demanded.

I dabbed at the wound in her forehead with my wet flannel. She shook her head impatiently.

'They recognized me, Frieda. Don't you understand?'

The implications appalled me.

'We must be careful,' she repeated. 'We must all be careful. If these monsters take over, none of us will be safe.'

I didn't know how to reassure her. 'You have nothing to be ashamed of,' I said, speaking more to myself than to her.

She was astonished at my words.

'I'm not ashamed,' she pointed out. 'I'm *afraid*. What are you talking about, Frieda?'

3

Soon after this incident, my Aunt Clara called me with more bad news.

'Your mother is ill,' she said, 'and you must come and visit her.'

I agreed, with an immediate clutch of anxiety, like a fist around my heart. I still blamed my mother for not protecting me against my father, but something in Clara's voice made that past grudge irrelevant.

I don't know what I expected. My mother was lying in the bedroom I had once slept in; the bed looked narrow and uncomfortable; the room itself dark and smaller even than I remembered. Her face on the pillow was ashen, and she was thin. It was her thinness that frightened me. When I took her wrist in my hand I could feel how light her bones were; the skin covered them loosely. There was something in the strange sweetish smell in the room which I could not place.

'Frieda,' she said feebly.

It was too much of an effort for her to lift her head off the pillow, and I bent to kiss her, aware again of that unfamiliar sickly smell.

I had brought some flowers, and my aunt took them away from me to put into a vase. Some tears formed at the back of my eyes. 'Are you in pain?' I asked, my voice seeming to come from a long way away, not from my own throat.

'Not now. The doctor has just given me an injection.'

'Does Father look after you?' I asked.

'When he is here he is very good,' she said.

I wondered if it was true.

'She needs a nurse,' said my aunt. 'You should be here, Frieda. Can't you see that?'

I could, but I had a sense of a trap that might close behind me. 'I will come in during the day,' I said, nevertheless, instinctively protecting myself.

My aunt nodded. 'That will help.'

Presently my mother fell asleep, and my aunt and I left her room and went into the kitchen. There I began to sob wildly, and my aunt embraced me with some approval. I was grieving for my mother's married suffering, quite as much as her illness, and also no doubt for myself.

'We must take turns,' I said, sensibly enough. 'I can't be here with my father.'

'He isn't often here,' said my aunt impatiently. 'She only imagines he is. I think he is in her head. She dreams a great deal.'

'In her head?' I repeated stupidly. 'Why should she dream of him? He was never kind to her.'

My aunt sighed. 'She likes to think he was,' she said. 'It may help her to think so. Anyway if he says one unkind thing to her while she is ill I will make him sorry.'

She sounded as fierce as if she had arranged for some gangster to beat him up, and I half believed she had; but she meant that she would do the job herself. Looking at her large, muscled arms and determined face it occurred to me that she was probably a match for him.

When my mother died I watched my father's grieving face and I wanted to scream at him: 'Why didn't you do something to make her life pleasanter while she was alive?' But I said nothing to him at all.

A little hardness came into my soul as I thought of my mother dreaming of his love and help. I said as much to my Aunt Clara after the funeral and she looked at me oddly.

'See it doesn't happen to you,' she said.

4

One afternoon I was in Lenya's flat when Weill brought the first definite news about negotiations with the owner of the Schiff-bauerdamm Theatre.

He came in very cold, from sitting on a bench outside the building where Brecht had been talking to Aufricht. Things had not gone well.

'I shall only have 25 per cent,' Weill told Lenya.

'But that is absurd,' said Lenya energetically, her eyes flashing and her teeth looking more wolfishly widespaced than ever.

'The director of the Schiff Theatre was difficult,' said Weill. 'He said they could use the eighteenth-century score.'

'How do you know things were difficult?' said Lenya.

'Brecht negotiated for me,' said Weill. 'He said so.'

They seemed suddenly to remember my presence and I smiled feebly.

'I'm sure Brecht wanted your music to be used,' I said, feeling comment was called for.

'He's not stupid,' said Lenya.

They both stared at me as if seeing me for a moment as an opponent.

'What about Bess Hauptmann?' asked Lenya.

'Only 12½ per cent,' said Weill.

I confess to some surprise at hearing that. I knew the amount of work that had gone into translating the original play. Moreover, two of the songs were altogether written by Bess.

'Poor Bess,' said Lenya. 'How badly she lets herself be treated.'

A little prickle, somewhere between satisfaction and alarm, filled me to hear as much, but I rooted out that ungracious thought with a frown. Lenya saw me frown and mistook the source. 'You can have a part, you can understudy me,' she suggested. The flattery of that offer took me by surprise.

'Really? Can I?'

'I'm never ill,' said Lenya grandly, 'so it isn't much of an offer.'

I remember then how she sang 'Pirate Jenny's Song', and how Brecht came in unannounced before she had finished. At the end of her song, he nodded, with his cigar in his mouth, and came over to change the direction of the palms of her hands. 'Not so Egyptian,' he said. 'Good. We can work on it.'

Brecht walked home with me along the warm, spring streets. The sky was dark and clear above us, and our feet knocked out hollow notes in the quiet. I think it was May, 1928. And I was filled with the simple happiness of having him at my side.

'I hear *Mahagonny* was a success,' I said.

'After the first shock,' he agreed. 'They were expecting more atonal music and instead the lights went up on Lenya dressed like a whore.'

And then he asked me closely, 'Has Lenya been making love to you?'

'Of course not,' I laughed.

He believed me.

'Have you been busy?'

I told him that Weill had set one of my songs to music and that I was going to try it out the next time there was a spot for me at Westerborg's. His eyes glittered shrewdly as he glanced sideways at me. On an impulse, I began to tell him about my mother's death, and he took my hand. His own mother, he told me, had died of cancer. He had found the pain too horrible to watch. 'It took so much suffering,' he mused, 'to turn her from a strong woman into someone who weighed no more than a child.'

I squeezed his hand comfortingly.

'We all need so much help,' he said.

His evident emotion melted me completely.

'The theatre has to be our family now,' he said.

And I thought about that. This new venture, this *Threepenny Opera*, this troupe I was joining. It was very much his family. His lovers. Bess Hauptmann had done so much of the writing; Weigel was playing the madam of the brothel; the stage was going to be designed by Casper Neher, and he was Brecht's childhood friend from the Augsburg days. We all belonged to him. I thought about that belonging. That night I was simply happy to be a part of his family. To have him at my side walking and talking as we had in the first days of love.

Brecht came home with me that night. He was exhilarated; talking of everything he planned. He wasn't directing the play, but he would be working on the set, writing new lines, intervening and perfecting.

'I shall have control,' he said, as we went up the stairs to my room.

'Control,' I said, opening the door, disliking the word which broke the tender mood.

'That's how to work,' he said impatiently.

'For the good of the group?' I asked.

'My little revolutionary,' he said, amused. 'Have you learnt some cattish ways, my little kitten?'

'I'm a human being,' I said savagely.

By this time he had a hand in my blouse.

'You don't care about the rest of us,' I said, weakening. I wanted him to share for a moment what he had made me feel.

'Have you been alone?' he asked me seriously. 'I hope so.'

'I have been without you,' I said.

He had his hand under my skirts by then, and I had no wish to explain anything.

The Shiffbauerdamm Theatre was an ornate nineteenth-century building in the centre of Berlin, owned by Aufricht, an actor much the same age as Brecht, with a rich father. Did we rehearse there? Rehearsals were what Brecht enjoyed most. It was how he liked to work, with people around and bustling; he had all his ideas then. Almost it might be said he did all his writing then. But the rehearsals for *The Threepenny Opera* were a special case. Everything about them was marked with a premonitory sense of impending disaster. It is hard now to imagine the fragmentary scenes from which the piece grew; its final form seems now so inevitable. I happened to be standing in the wings one afternoon when I heard Hauptmann ask where Brecht was and Weigel, her face always like a mask in repose, explained he was with Carola Neher. 'He is writing new lines for her,' she said.

Carola Neher was playing Polly Peachum. She was a woman of such extraordinary beauty that other women lost all their vividness when she stood by them. In the first days of rehearsal she had gone off to be with her sick husband. Now he had died; and she was back, dressed in black and shining with glamour.

It was obvious to anyone that she was Brecht's new and favourite woman, but I was surprised to see Hauptmann's eyes close with pain as she heard that Brecht was coaching his new pupil. With astonishment I registered that she was in the grip of terrible jealousy.

I consulted my own feelings, and found no pain whatsoever. I had come through some strange ordeal, it seemed. By asking for so much less, I now could bear far more. I even took a little satisfaction in the discomfiture of my rival.

Hauptmann asked Weigel, 'Do you think he will marry her when the divorce comes through?'

That there was to be a divorce, I knew. Weigel did not reply, only smiled. I was astonished at the intensity in Hauptmann's voice, and the pain in her face, and I realized that she still imagined she could have Brecht for herself alone as if he were an ordinary man. I knew better than that; I no longer even asked myself if it was better to ask so little. I knew at least it reduced pain.

When Brecht came back on stage, leading Carola to the place he thought she should be, Weigel approached him with confidence.

'Listen,' she said to him. 'I have an idea. I could play this madam of a brothel as a woman with no legs.'

Brecht always listened to Weigel as if her ideas were the only ones he could trust. As if he were in awe of her theatrical imagination. 'You mean as a woman who does not exist from the waist down?' he asked her.

She nodded. 'Exactly . . . I could be brought onstage in a wheelchair.'

He liked the idea, but before this could be resolved there was a little diversion. One of the most famous singers of cabaret was in the show, Rosa Valetti. I had always envied her gifts, and loved her daring raunchy style. It was all the more astonishing that she should go up to Brecht and refuse to sing one of the ballads. I remember it was that famous ballad of sexual obsession which

63

Hauptmann had written, and when Rosa Valetti refused to sing it because it was filthy, I saw Hauptmann throw up her hands in despair. She need not have worried. Lenya took the sheets from Valetti and sang it instead.

It is a marvellous song, about the way a man's toughness is fatally reduced by his need for sex from women. That was the moment when that other song was born, the one that had still to be written, the one that became my theme song. About women's complementary and equally destructive need. To love and nurture and endure. And the damage it did us.

I sat drinking bad coffee with Bess Hauptmann next morning in a café not far from the Schiff. She looked thin; her hair, which was usually glossy, had a wispy look to it. She had both hands on the coffee cup and they were trembling. It was a warm summer day, though the sky was white and overcast; and there were beads of sweat on her upper lip, which she removed from time to time with the tip of her finger.

'I'm short of sleep,' she explained. 'Last night I worked right through. Typing up the latest alterations.'

'Why do that?' I asked indignantly.

'I don't want him to find another typist,' she said with a melancholy smile.

I recognized her wish to be indispensable.

'You must be worried about the play,' I prompted, since she seemed disinclined to say any more.

She shrugged, and I could tell that the success of the play was not her first worry that morning.

'He promised to marry me,' she said after a pause. 'You know that, don't you?'

I made some noncommittal noise.

'Did he ever say as much to you?' she demanded.

'No,' I replied, honestly enough.

That pleased her, and she drank her coffee to the dregs with an abrupt gesture, nodding her head. It was clear that if she went on working as she did she would have a nervous collapse.

'All right for Weigel,' she kept saying.

I didn't understand what she could mean.

'Weigel can always find work. Doesn't have to be on the stage. There's the radio. There's films,' said Bess. 'For a woman to make a life for herself as a writer is impossible.'

I wasn't sure I agreed with that. But Hauptmann seemed to be looking for some material explanation which could justify her submission to Brecht's needs.

'How old are you?' she asked me.

'Nearly eighteen,' I said.

She sighed. 'Lucky girl. You can still do anything with your life. Meet an ordinary man. Marry. Have children.'

None of that sounded very attractive to me that summer morning but I could see Hauptmann was very gloomy at the contrast between us.

'Weigel has a child,' she said. 'Someone looks after him. She arranged things very well for herself.'

I ate the cherries from my tart one by one, not knowing how to reply. And then, I don't know why, I asked her something that had been bothering me for weeks.

'This play. Have you made sure your name is on it?'

'These things don't matter,' she said.

I raised my eyebrows.

'I'm a Socialist,' she explained. 'I don't have any interest in bourgeois ideas of property.'

I wasn't sure what to say.

'In any case, he transforms what he touches,' she said heavily. 'When I write I only imitate him.'

'You wrote the Alabama song,' I pointed out. 'It's one of the ones Weill particularly liked. That was very successful.'

'Listen to me,' she said, changing tack. 'If you write about sex it's better to have a man's name to protect you. Remember that if you write songs for yourself one day.'

Since I had already done as much, I remained silent. I was too young to articulate what was obvious. She was trying to find an excuse for allowing herself to be exploited.

If I could see so clearly what was happening to Bess Hauptmann, it might be thought that I could see as much for myself. Not in the least. For one thing, it seemed to me that my situation was quite

65

different. I needed much less: smiles, friendship, education, visits from time to time, some sex. These I largely had. That my whole emotional being was centred on a man for whom I was only a creature at the periphery of his life seemed a choice I was happy to make. I had tried to break free once; unfree, I was content. There seemed no exploitation in this. On the contrary, I felt privileged. I had a sense, as the rehearsals proceeded with increasing violence, that I was part of something so exciting that my life afterwards could only be pale in comparison.

Rehearsals went on until late at night, exhaustingly. A small jazz group had been hired. Weill's music coloured my days. I had a minor role as one of the girls in the brothel. This gave me a great deal of time to sit around and listen to what people were saying. Brecht was not the director but took over furiously if anyone spoke the words of an earlier version. He insisted on rewriting lines that did not work and this meant the actors had to keep relearning their parts. He had a savage tongue for their mistakes: 'You can't act. Can't think. Can't move,' he would say to them. 'No more than a piece of shit.'

There were grumbles of revolt among the cast. Their indignation increased whenever Brecht chose to sit with the lovely Carola Neher, instructing her while the rest of the cast waited around.

I never saw him shout at Weigel. One day I was sitting at the side of the stage when Weigel sat down heavily on a chair, pressing her hand into one side of her belly.

'You seem to be in pain,' I questioned cautiously.

There was something formidable about her that made it impossible to chatter. She nodded, looking ashen under her normally rather sallow skin. 'Here,' she said, holding her side.

'It might be appendicitis,' I said uneasily. My mother had always been a hypochondriac about that possibility.

'I feel sick,' she muttered, standing up and hurrying off.

I followed anxiously and could hear her vomiting before she reached the dressing room. I was now thoroughly alarmed. 'Let me call a doctor.'

'No,' she said ferociously. 'I shall be all right.'

66

And on stage it was impossible to guess if she was suffering.

About a week before the show was to open the weather grew unbearably hot. It was a close, oppressive August heat that frayed everyone's temper. The director's frustration brought perspiration to his face. His own feelings were clearly with the actors, and he approached Carola and Brecht to suggest that they should go off to another room so the rest of the rehearsal could proceed.

Carola was a marvellously beautiful creature of a violent temper and as the director made his tentative, almost timorous, suggestion she flared up at him.

'Nobody talks to me like that,' she said.

The director, already regretting the risk he had taken, mopped his forehead with his handkerchief and, seeing his dismay, she flung the script she had been relearning at his feet. The director blanched at the anger in her eyes.

'Do the part yourself,' she said crudely, and walked off the stage.

There was general consternation. A buzz of voices considered the unlikelihood of finding anyone to play her part at such short notice. And we were opening in a week. Bess Hauptmann's face however, I remember particularly. It was impassive and silent with just a trace of satisfaction on her lips even though the risk to the play that was half hers was plain.

I don't remember exactly how Brecht came to be in my rooms one night. I see him lying on my bed in a vest, his arms behind his head. I came and lay next to him, and he comforted himself by putting his face between my breasts.

'So small and round,' he sighed. 'Everything young is sweet.'

I pressed his hot face against me, looking down with a certain satisfaction at my pert and delicate breasts. Even Carola Neher for all her beauty might not have such firm flesh.

'You give me no trouble,' he said.

I was flattered by that thought, and held him more tightly. 'Does Bess give you trouble?' I asked.

He sighed and did not answer. 'You understand what I need,' he said.

67

I put my face into his hair, which smelled as acrid as a sweaty animal, and he stroked my flanks.

'I am tired,' he said.

'You seem worried too. Is it the show?' I asked him.

'It is Helli,' he said. 'She is ill.'

I wondered if the pain she had ignored had been appendicitis.

'I took her to the hospital this evening,' he said. 'I shall have to write her out of the show.'

And then he felt my tense belly reflectively. 'You don't have an inch of fat,' he said approvingly.

Make love to me, I wanted to call out to him, longing for his fingers to move downwards. But he seemed to be searching for comfort rather than sex.

'I must sleep for a couple of hours,' he said, and closed his eyes.

As soon as he closed his eyes, he was asleep. I drew myself up into a sitting position and looked down on his pale defenceless face. He is like a child, I thought protectively, gently stroking his hair, and adjusting my body the better to hold him. Like a child, he slept when he wanted and woke at his need, and the household adjusted its rhythms around him. I wasn't sleepy, but I lay at his side, unwilling to move until the first light of morning came through the window at four o'clock and I heard him stir and move off to pee.

'Are you all right?' I called after him.

'I'm fine,' he said. 'I'll go now.'

Hearing this, I was horribly disappointed. I had kept off sleep for something better. He saw as much and patted my head, smiling. 'Bess and I have a great deal to do before rehearsals begin,' he explained.

I felt the snub painfully. 'Did you only come for a rest?' I asked.

At this he frowned, and I cursed my rashness. I had no wish to make demands on him. He had enough demands made on him. But he smiled after a moment, forgivingly. 'I came to lie on your sweet breast,' he said, and kissed me on the forehead.

It must have been the next morning that I found myself sitting in Lenya's flat rehearsing some of her numbers in case she should fall ill. That at least was the avowed purpose of my visit. I soon realized she had something else in mind. Her face was alight with angry animation; her mouth widening all the while she talked; her eyes flashing as she raged up and down the room like a leopard pacing his cage.

'Why are you such a little fool?' she kept saying. 'There must be so many men in the world for you. It makes me sick to watch you sitting at the side of a stage looking on. Like a voyeur. As if you had no other rights.'

I thought she was talking about the size of my part, but it soon became clear she was not.

'You have admirers,' she said. 'They come and sit and look at you.' There was always an audience at rehearsals; a number of eminent writers were curious to know what Brecht would do. I could not think they had come to admire me. It soon appeared she was talking about Wilhelm, who sometimes hung around the entrance to the theatre.

'No one I care about,' I said.

She sighed, and came and sat very close to me. I was in a strange state from the frustrations of the night before, and when she put her hand on my knee the strength of my own response was alarming.

'There,' she said. 'What you need is so simple. Why give yourself such pain?'

I could not catch my breath enough to reply, as her fingers unbuttoned my blouse.

'Don't,' I said feebly, as one hand cupped my breast, and another felt its way downwards. Her face came closer to mine; her breath was acrid with tobacco, and for a moment I saw her huge mouth as ugly and frightening; especially the flash of white square teeth. Then her fingers loosened my skirt and found a way towards my crotch.

'Damn,' I said, to her amusement, as the first wave of pleasure lifted me. And then we both slid to the floor, twining about one another's bodies like snakes, until at last we both lay exhausted on her Afghan rug.

'That is something I've been wanting to do,' said Lenya, 'for a long time.'

Thinking about the incident later in the day, it seemed curiously unworrying. It was sex without any emotional attachment; lust without even the pretence of love, and as such altogether irrelevant. Later that day I was to receive a conventional offer of love.

Coming out of the theatre, I found Wilhelm standing waiting for me, and he grabbed my hand as I turned towards my home. 'I must speak to you,' he said.

I wasn't completely surprised, but I was tired, so I said, 'We have nothing to talk about, have we?'

'I've been following you,' he said. 'You must have noticed. I have something to tell you.'

He was a simple, solid-faced man, not without charm but utterly unattractive to me. He was dressed more carefully than I remembered him; or perhaps it seemed so since I had accustomed myself to Brecht's slovenliness; certainly he had a fresh shirt and pressed trousers, and there was an almost military quality to his stance.

'You must have a new job,' I said.

'Yes,' he nodded. 'My life is altogether changed. And now I realize you were the most important girl to enter my life. I'm in love with you. I want to take you out of your sleazy nightclub life.'

'But I love this life,' I said.

'You could be pure again,' he said. 'I could give you a home. You wouldn't need to show your body for men to gape at, or sing for an audience.'

He stopped and took my hands and looked down at me with a sudden sentimental expression that horrified me. 'You could sing to your own children,' he said.

'That would bore me,' I replied.

He was furious, and for a moment I thought he would hit me. 'That is a completely decadent thing to say,' he shouted at me.

'Wilhelm,' I said with a certain compassion, 'why should you suddenly imagine you love me?'

He looked depressed at the question. 'I always liked you,' he said. 'Now I can see what a pearl I threw away.'

'You didn't throw me away. I left you for Brecht,' I reminded him.

'That lout,' he said. 'I don't know how you can let him put his hands on you. He smells and dresses like a docker.'

70

'What is wrong with being a worker?' I asked.

'And let me tell you, this show is going to be a disaster,' he continued. 'Everyone says so. It will fold after three days.'

There I thought he might be right, but I detached myself from him, still embarrassed by the softness in his brown eyes.

'Let me look after you,' he said.

'It's not what I want,' I said firmly.

The dress rehearsal opened dangerously. Brecht insisted the electrical equipment be visible to the audience; he shouted at the stage hands while the director would have preferred to get on rehearsing the actors. The clothes had been inexpensive, and were still being improved. My own costume pleased me, I have to say. My aunt had used clever needlework to enhance the cheap material and made it fall more sensuously round my figure; I knew the colours made me as magnetic as Lenya herself once I took my position on the stage. If Brecht himself was too busy to notice, I drew a flattering pat from the director.

Macheath, Mack the Knife, was being played by Paulsen, a popular actor who had always had doubts about risking his career on the part. He came on stage that day in a double-breasted black suit and white spats, with a sword cane under his arm. Brecht circled round him cautiously. It was not the dress he had imagined for a gangster.

'These aren't the clothes we designed,' said Brecht.

'No, they are my own,' Paulsen said serenely. He was pleased with his own appearance.

'And what inspiration made you decide on a sky-blue cravat?' asked Brecht, with an edge to his voice.

'Do you like it?' asked Paulsen.

'It's absurd. You look completely bourgeois,' snapped Brecht. 'Get out of those clothes.'

Paulsen smiled, knowing his withdrawal would ensure that the show was a complete flop. 'I won't go on in the rags you found for me,' he asserted calmly.

Brecht stared at him. 'A bourgeois gangster,' he repeated and then, to everyone's surprise, sidled away towards the piano.

The rest of the cast shifted uneasily as Brecht leant over the piano, talking to Weill. When Brecht came back again we could not believe our luck. Another catastrophe had been averted.

'Let's get on,' said Brecht.

And so rehearsal proceeded.

That was how Brecht and Weill came to write the famous Moritat for Mack the Knife, that ambiguous, sexy tribute to the world of fine clothes and hidden brutality in which we were all living.

Through most of the last weeks, Weill had been the least agitated of us all. Precise as he was in his music, he was indifferent to the tensions on stage. Sometimes, on the hottest days, when his bald head shone, it was as if his eyes disappeared behind their thick glass protection, and it was impossible to tell how he felt. All the more surprising then that last day to hear him bellowing with fury. 'Outrageous. Unbelievable. Everything must stop,' he shouted.

Lotte Lenya's name had been left off the programme. There was no reason for it, and no way of putting it right before the opening. The sight of his fury unnerved us. Only Lenya herself could soothe him, and she got down from the stage to do so. The rehearsal went on, unevenly, often interrupted, and with frequent spurts of Brecht's anger, until Lenya had to sing her Pirate song. She was still soothing Kurt, and Brecht suddenly seemed to remember me. He frowned, appraised, and smiled.

'Stand in,' he said.

And that was how I came to sing a song of Lenya's for the first time on any stage. As I sang I watched her face, where she sat close to her husband in the half-darkness, and wondered how she felt to hear my voice hit the same notes. She had an opera voice in those days that was finer than mine; I already had smoky, growling notes in my voice that I had learnt not from Lenya herself but American black voices. It was my own version therefore I sang, and I hit the notes truly, so that when I had finished there was a little ripple of applause from that hardened audience, stressed as it was.

Naturally, Lenya sang on the opening night.

5

Some nights enter the memory like a dream. So it is, I remember, the lights went up on that white half-curtain as the hand organist began to play the grinding accompaniment to 'Mack the Knife'. There was darkness in the auditorium. Lenya stood next to me clutching my hand. She was trembling and white, and perspiration covered her neck. I could tell she was in the grip of stage fright. I gave her an encouraging kiss on her naked shoulder, and could smell perspiration under the powder as she squeezed my fingers. For ever afterwards that mix of sweat and powder meant animal fear to me, and I always respond with gentleness to it. She was dressed in black stockings, torn at the knee, and at that moment she looked like a sad creature of the streets; ugly, thin, hopeless.

Most of us were anxious. It was possible to see the audience through a slit in the curtains, and I could see they were well dressed and quiet; not the kind to show approval of gangsters and whores. As the jaunty song ground out, I could just make out their stony faces. Brecht, too, for all his usual coolness, had an unlit cigar in his mouth and a face sallow with worry. The Peachums went on first, and there were a few laughs for them; then Lenya went on and sang her first song. I could hear an ambiguous stilling in the audience, and Brecht, at my side now, mumbled with a certain bitter satisfaction that at least she had frightened them. The rest of us wondered, looking out over the ranks of silent faces, whether these comfortable people came to the theatre to be frightened.

The turning point came with the Cannon song, which the police chief sang with Macheath. It is a song in praise of military life, with a bloodcurdling delight in slaughter; its most famous line speaks of chopping natives into beefsteak tartare. And the audience loved it. The jolly tune had them stamping in rhythm.

73

They wouldn't stop clapping until Macheath and the chief of police were compelled to come out and sing it again. Were they delighted with those ingenious rhymes, and the comradeship bounce of the song? I doubt if they recognized the satirical bite. The men were remembering army days and the camaraderie of war. And soon I was on stage with my hip well out as Lenya had taught me, sidling about the stage and staring at an audience smiling with glee even at our brothel. It was clear that the women loved Macheath's brutality.

The tunes repeated, the applause mounted, and the fragments became a whole. The show was a success. At the final curtain Lenya's face was transformed; perhaps we were all transfigured. Lenya looked as if she had just reached a climax of pleasure. The sweat had washed most of the powder from her smooth cheeks. Her skin glowed. Perhaps I looked the same. We bowed, and the audience clapped, and next day the 'Sold Out' notices went up at the box office.

Within a few days Brecht bought a new car, and a great many new clothes. The rest of us had no such obvious change in our living conditions, but my own career was also assured in its modest way from that time onwards. All of us had become fashionable. I was offered jobs in films, and not only German films; a Hollywood producer invited me to the United States. I sang on the radio for a large sum of money. And I too bought things: handbags, silk scarves, good shoes, a fur coat. I took a larger flat.

Brecht's new clothes resembled his old ones; his shirts were now handmade, but he wore them with as little care to seem well dressed. And those ubiquitous leather jackets still looked like those worn by the working classes, even though they were so much more expensively cut.

He had nevertheless become a celebrity. I knew that, and indeed when I ran into Wilhelm in the street a few weeks later I could not resist saying as much with some pride, since Wilhelm had always spoken of him with such contempt.

'He stole translations from François Villon and Kipling,' Wilhelm sneered. 'The reviewers say so.'

'He doesn't believe in literary property,' I replied angrily.

'It's the music people love,' said Wilhelm and, as if to prove the point, someone passing us on the pavement went by whistling 'Mack the Knife'. I was so angered at this that we had walked some way along the street together before I became aware that Wilhelm had a small Nazi pin in his jacket. Seeing as much, I stopped. 'You are a Nazi?' I asked incredulously.

'I can't bear what I see every day in the streets,' he said, withdrawing his hand and perhaps remembering I was Jewish. 'We have to do something. While you and your decadent crew enjoy yourselves, people are starving.'

'I can't believe you really hope for something good from Hitler,' I said, my eyes searching his face.

'Do you trust the Left?' he demanded.

'It seems a decent option,' I said after a moment.

'Your Marxist reading,' he sneered.

'All this violence in the streets,' I said heavily. 'The Nazis are terrorists.'

He looked uncomfortable, and explained that he had met Goebbels recently at a party and found him graceful and fascinating.

'Don't you have any doubts?' I asked coldly.

I did not want to remind him of my own Jewish inheritance. It was very important to me psychologically to be with a group of people who opposed Hitler on grounds less personal than that.

6

About this time, Brecht moved from his Spigernstrasse apartment to something grander, and soon afterwards he married Helene Weigel.

I heard the news from Bess Hauptmann, who had called me in her despair. She too had moved; but she had not yet arranged her new apartment; and she had entered so deep a depression that unwashed cups and glasses still clustered on her tables and even on the carpet. As I listened, I did not move to carry those dishes to the kitchen, though the thought that I ought to do so bothered me awkwardly. My own pain seemed at a distance. I did not seem to own it. I was no more than a witness of Bess's suffering. And mainly I felt protective. Her black hair lay dank, her face was depleted, and her always slender form looked almost skeletal. He has devoured her, I thought. He has eaten her up.

'I can't understand,' Bess kept saying. 'Why not Carola Neher? At least she is beautiful.'

I said it was very surprising. I was still stunned by the extent of Brecht's duplicity.

'I never saw Weigel as a rival,' Bess repeated stupidly.

I agreed she seemed plain and ordinary offstage.

'He tells me nothing will change between us,' she said, and her voice caught on the pathos of hope. 'He says Weigel knows he can't live without other women.'

I imagined in that she was right. Probably Brecht would have to give up almost nothing as a result of marrying her.

'Of course, she is his mother. He can live like a pampered child,' Bess continued. 'Well fed. Comfortable.'

Her voice had hit a low monotone. We were both drinking, and my thoughts wandered. I patted her hand, and began to think of my own situation. Would anything change for me?

'Don't you wonder how she bears it?' Bess asked. 'She knows

76

the only way to stay close to Brecht is to give and give and give and ask nothing. And she can do that, because she has her own inner resource.'

'And you?'

'No,' she said.

And what of my own feelings that night? I made myself some toast, buttered it, and did not eat it. Then I went and sat for a while in the darkness of the bedroom. I had chosen a coverlet for the bed which matched the curtains; a luxurious green and purple patterned brocade which caught the starlight through the window strangely; I stared out at the stars. I remembered Orion.

By my bedside table sat the books I had been reading. I switched on the light there, and so extinguished the stars. I looked at the pattern on the light shade. I liked the colours of the room in the electric light. I liked the way I had folded my clothes on the new white shelves. I have my life in order, I thought.

And then the pain began. He would have no time for me. He would no longer need me. I should be on my own for weeks at a time, waiting, and he would never come. Or when he came he would be preoccupied.

I went to the bathroom, intending to shower and go to bed. The shower was a new pleasure for me. I loved the way the hot spiky jets made the blood course round my body. I liked their pressure on my face. I went to the taps to test the hotness of the water, and there caught a vision of myself in the bathroom mirror. I looked old and ugly. My face was drawn, and my lips turned downwards. My eyes were huge and doomed like a cow's, I thought, waiting to be taken to slaughter. I threw a flannel at the vision, hating myself and my face equally. I did not bother to run the shower.

I had a small collection of records in those days. There was a Mozart piano concerto, with a marvellous lifting tune that I particularly loved; I played it right through, waiting for the emotions that usually followed, finding only a far-off echo of them, as if even that beauty could only reach me at a distance. And then I began to comfort myself.

He had not been treacherous to me. He had never offered marriage. He had never offered fidelity. I could accommodate myself to the new situation. I could go on as before. There would be no problem going on as before.

And a great weight lifted from my heart. I went to bed and slept without dreaming.

The next day I heard that Bess Hauptmann had tried to take her own life, that she had eaten pills, finished the gin bottle, had to have her stomach washed out.

I seemed to know the news before it was given to me.

Some time after this my aunt and I took a weekend off. We hired a chauffeur and a car and set off through the countryside towards the seaside. It was an autumn day; the beech trees and maples were burning as red as tigers and there was a kind of yellow light everywhere. I sat in a haze of beauty. When we got to the seaside town, we walked up and down the sea road, and watched the blue sky that had fallen into the mud, and the birds that sat on the edges of those blue puddles and set off in whirring flocks. I observed the birds only flew with their own kind. The sun shone in their white feathers.

'It's enough to make you believe in something,' said my aunt dreamily.

'It's nothing more than natural beauty,' I said. 'No need to explain it all with God, that I can see.'

'Don't be so clever,' said my aunt sharply. 'There are worse deceptions than that one. Now, I want to talk to you very seriously. Do you still see Brecht? I mean as a lover?'

'Not often,' I said.

'Often or not,' she said impatiently, 'it's all one. What's the matter with you? You earn your own money, don't you? Good money now.'

I agreed that was so.

'Why do you need him?' she then asked simply.

I had no answer.

'Find someone else,' said my aunt. 'Pull yourself together. It's time to make a break.'

'I can't,' I said.

'You're afraid to try,' she said vigorously. 'Why wait until he tells you to go?'

'He won't do that,' I said confidently. 'He never does let go of the people he loves. It's not his way.'

The white light on the sea filled me with such optimism that I said as much with perfect serenity, and was astonished when my aunt rounded on me.

'He spits and farts. I think he's disgusting.'

'Brecht's personal habits are no concern of yours,' I said loftily.

'And he doesn't bath much,' she said.

'I don't object.'

'Why should a lovely young girl like you be part of his harem?' she demanded. 'At his beck and call, once a month if he feels like it?'

'Why, how often do you see your M. Barbusse?' I retorted.

She smiled at the note of spite in my voice, and began to explain that everything had changed; the divorce proceedings were in train; she would soon be a legal wife after so many years.

'Are you sure of that?' I asked.

She was hurt, rather than angry, at my doubts. 'I have never been a sentimental fool like you,' she pointed out. 'I make sure of what is happening to me.'

'I don't need to be married,' I said.

That night in the narrow, cold bed of the boarding house we had chosen, I lay and thought how best to adjust my life sensibly. I did not seriously consider giving up Brecht altogether. Nor was I interested in finding some kind of supplementary lover. Yet what was I hoping for?

Hauptmann survived her suicide attempt, and I observed without surprise that she did not finish with him either.

PART THREE

POLITICS

'What keeps mankind alive? The fact that millions
Are daily tortured, stifled, punished, silenced,
                                        oppressed . . .'

Brecht: The second finale of *The Threepenny Opera*

1

I am not sure when I joined the Communist Party.

Bess joined long before me; Weigel too was already a member. The poor of the city lay about the streets, the shoeless, hopeless children of Weimar's unemployed. I had seen them through my growing up. Those pavements were always waiting for me. I could still remember the bite of hunger even in the days when I travelled by car, met the cold in a fur coat, and ate at good restaurants with white linen around my neck. Yet I did not join only out of compassion. There was a shiver of fear too. We felt the breath of something sinister, something that had to be fought, that we were all fighting, and that had its evil yellow eye for that reason upon us.

Against that monster, the Communist Party seemed the only reliable ally. And its certainties seemed a protection. Looking back now, I see that my loyalties were all of a piece with my devotion to the Brecht workshop: for both the Party and for Brecht I was willing to serve, while earning my money elsewhere. It was the strength of the demand that seemed to ensnare me. And there was no shortage of violence on the streets to make the point for me that the present society in which we lived could not last. I was with Brecht one morning, driven in his car up to barricades, when police fired on demonstrators who were part of the strikes.

Brecht was at that time astronomically rich, since *The Threepenny Opera* was earning money all over Europe. I believe he was already saving money in a Swiss bank account. I too was no longer poor, and was wearing a new fur coat when we stopped at those barricades. Both of us nevertheless saw ourselves as aligned with those who protested against the conditions in which people of the city were living through that winter. We were certain it was the system that was at fault and not just the Germans. If America, that wonderland of goods and gaiety, could crash that 1929, if there were millions of unemployed there as well as in Germany, then it was clear that capitalism itself was responsible.

My allegiance was simple enough to understand. Brecht's too; though he never became a card-carrying member of the Party. I think I joined after the events surrounding the production of *Mahagonny* in Leipzig. And that play puzzled me, for all the crooning sadness of Weill's music. The songs were poems of Bess Hauptmann and their words perplexed me. What was this Bilbao we were to long for? And what was the city of Mahagonny? I remember asking Brecht something about the title at least, and he replied from a great distance, 'Mahagonny. The dream of the petit bourgeoisie. The cosy world of gin shops and gaming tables. If it ever takes over in Germany, I'm off.' At the time I don't think he felt seriously menaced.

By then I was always part of the team, even if I was on the periphery of Brecht's life. Bess was too. And even when Weigel was there, he made no secret of his sexual interest in other young members of the company. I liked to watch him work with Weigel. She was a rock throughout the production; and we had need of something strong and fixed, since right from the beginning the play was threatened by disturbances directed against Jews and Communists alike.

It was during the rehearsals of *Mahagonny* that I asked Lenya about her own marriage. 'Doesn't Kurt mind what you do?' I asked her.

'He knows all about it. It's a relief for him,' she said. 'You know when he is working hard he really doesn't need a woman.'

'Isn't he jealous then?' I asked.

'Of course not. He loves the piano first and then me. In any case, I don't deceive him. I tell him everything. Whoever loves Brecht has to have the same temperament,' she said.

I was silent.

'Maybe he and you should get together,' I said sullenly. 'Then the rest of us who are less voracious could be happy.'

She laughed. 'Another reason why we leave one another alone.' Her knowing words alarmed me. I was afraid, with that ripple of prescience which in country legends denotes someone stepping on a future grave.

When we arrived in Leipzig, there were already marchers with placards in the square before the theatre. We had been categorized as decadent in advance; now we were threatened as Jews and Communists. And the threat was violent. Kurt went to visit his father, who was still a cantor in that city, and was by no means sure that it was safe to invite him to the opening night. Weigel was the bravest of us all; she had no physical fear. Threats made her stronger. She talked only of staging and technique.

The first night we knew we were going to have trouble. It was not only a question of demonstrators outside the theatre, there were a number of perfectly suited Nazis in the audience. Looking down at rows of them in the stalls, they reminded me of insects working in unselfish obedience. Among them sat Weill's father, looking particularly and vulnerably Jewish.

I don't know what Brecht expected, or what any of us thought could come of that performance. There were shouts and blows as soon as the curtain went up. Weill's father was felled by a casual thug. The play broke up in disorder and was taken off after three days.

All this made my own allegiance to communism seem logical. There was another strand, however. I remember walking through a cemetery in south Germany with Brecht some time after this, while he told me about his play *The Measures Taken*, and how much the Party would dislike it; it is a teaching play about a comrade who is willing to accept his own death once he is persuaded that it is necessary. He told the story with one of his most ambiguous grins; and I responded instantly with that masochistic wish to serve which has activated the religious spirit through the ages. It brought a ripple of excitement to the back of my neck as if I were reading a poem, and even as I responded I was horrified. Am I a natural martyr? I asked myself. And my spirit tried uneasily to repudiate the implications of that thrill of pleasure. Nevertheless, I had no qualms about the Party.

By the end of March 1930, the German constitution had been suspended; the Communists and Social Democrats were still feuding; we were left to argue among ourselves about whether it was possible for the two great parties of the Left to work together. The next elections saw the end of Weimar.

85

Meanwhile, Brecht was an industry of his own, and we were his workers. I remember he adapted a novel of Maxim Gorky – *Mother* – into a play, and rehearsed it for performance downstairs in Aufricht's theatre, while upstairs Weill rehearsed a chorus line for another *Mahagonny* production. It took some courage for us to play in *Mother* and sing songs in praise of communism at a time when Nazi thugs ruled the streets, but none of us refused. It was part of the fight; and the fight was going on. It did not yet occur to any of us that the fight would be lost, or that we ought to be safeguarding ourselves by leaving the country.

Bess Hauptmann and I were part of a piece of street theatre in a poor northern suburb when I felt myself in physical danger for the first time. It was a quiet, sunny evening. Just in front of me, on the pavement, a housewife jiggled an infant in a pram. The child's bottle had fallen to the ground and I picked it up and surreptitiously wiped it. Along the street was a market where people could exchange household goods for food. I remember a slight irritation at the distracting bustle.

I was there to lead the song and when the time came for that, and we stood singing with clasped hands, I became aware that stallholders and customers alike had fallen silent. A number of young Nazis had marched along the market street and their uniforms soon made a solid band around us. Our rally had been largely among women workers from a local textile factory; they were ill-fed and scared; and our song petered out before its triumphal chorus.

My heart began to bang loudly in my chest as I swiftly counted the uniforms: they were twice our number. One of the few men among the factory workers, a thickset peasant in appearance, motioned the women to one side and approached the Nazi leader, who looked no more than sixteen. Before the man could speak, however, a brick caught him on the side of his head and he fell to his knees. One or two more bricks followed, and women began to scream. Bess and I began to run away along the street farthest from the stalls. Behind us was the sound of breaking glass, and laughter.

As I ran, someone snatched at the bag in my hand. In my terror, some instinctive obstinacy made me try to hold on to it, and in a moment I was tripped. I remember lying on the pavement, crying with helplessness and anger as other people ran past me. What distressed me was the casual opportunism of the foot that had tripped me and the hand that had snatched at my purse: it was the true spirit of Weimar Berlin.

That I had lost the bag disturbed me less. I had money at home. I was not especially short of money in those days. My income came from the cabaret appearances and the records I made of my own songs. The new politics had begun to enter those; but they were still closer in feel to American blues singers; I enjoyed the irony of protesting about the treatment of women in a world dominated by men, while continuing to serve Brecht.

Very occasionally now, Brecht would visit me in my satin-sheeted bed. He no longer praised my youth. Indeed, I was seven years older than that sixteen-year-old girl he had first pressed himself against in the woods of Berlin. Still, my body was firm, and he made love to me as sweetly as ever he had. He was very insistent that we give one another the most intense sexual pleasure, and to this end used great ingenuity. It was the basis of the relationship. I understood that, and did not raise the question of my own emotional needs.

Nevertheless, I could not prevent myself asking him, in a husky voice, whether he still needed me.

'Of course I need you. We all need you,' he replied impatiently.

It was not quite the answer I had wished to hear.

One day my aunt came to see me dressed in unusually discreet, well-cut street clothes, and announced she was leaving Germany. 'You should go too while there is time,' she said.

'I can't,' I explained.

'You have the money. You won't have a passport problem. I have arranged everything with Barbusse. You can come to Switzerland.'

'I can't,' I repeated.

'Why not?' she asked me.

'I can't leave Brecht,' I replied.

I had never put it to myself so baldly.

The fact was that everything I valued had come together. My love, my sexual needs, my working life, my politics: they all connected back to the same figure of a man, who was the lynchpin. If he were removed, I was sure the whole structure of my life would fall in pieces.

'You are absolutely mad,' said my aunt. 'I will argue with you no more.'

2

It was natural for me to try and learn Russian on political grounds; perhaps I also hoped to make myself necessary to Brecht in his dealings with the Soviet Union. In doing so, I made my next move more likely. We do not always recognize the doors that close upon us, even as we miss the doors that open.

It happened like this. We were invited to a party in the apartment of a rich friend in honour of Sergei Tretyakov, the Russian playwright. He had come to Germany interested in German theatre productions and was trawling for those who could help the spread of world communism. He was a tall thin balding figure, with good German, who took the centre of any stage without difficulty.

We had come straight from rehearsal in a group; Brecht, Weigel, Bess and I. And Brecht found himself on the periphery of the gathering and did not like it. He refused to go over to be introduced to the guest of honour, and stood with his back to the wall, looking sullen, until someone close to Tretyakov recognized him and whispered as much to the Russian.

Tretyakov came over to Brecht immediately.

If Brecht was mollified by this show of respect, it did not make him more complaisant, and I was soon astonished to hear him arguing with Tretyakov about Party policy. Brecht disapproved of Stalin's hostility to working with Social Democrats, even though both Bess and Weigel frequently justified it. The argument grew heated and rancorous, and I marvelled at Tretyakov's willingness to continue the conversation. I suppose now that Brecht was one of the key figures he had been sent by the Comintern to recruit, and he had no choice but to placate and charm, even though Brecht's insistence on local German issues closely resembled the views of the exiled Trotsky.

A few days later, Brecht happened to mention casually that he

89

had some letters from Russia that he needed translating into German. Would I help him? I was delighted to try. He suggested that I come round to his apartment for supper with Weigel and himself the following day to receive them. If I was disappointed not to have him come to my flat, I concealed the emotion and agreed to turn up for the evening meal at eight. It was rare enough for Weigel to be at home in the evening; and I treated the invitation as a sign of becoming a closer part of his family life.

I rang the bell without trepidation, carrying a Russian dictionary, and a typewriter in case he wanted me to do something after we had eaten. Weigel answered the door with a quizzical expression, and I saw at once that I was not expected.

'Brecht invited me,' I explained, my heart for some reason beginning to bang unpleasantly.

'I see,' she said. 'Well, come in. He isn't here.'

Pleasant smells came from the kitchen as we walked along the passage into the living room. It was clear that I had come when Weigel expected to eat. A handsome young boy in pyjamas appeared briefly; a buxom young serving woman caught him and led him away.

'Did Brecht invite you to eat?' Weigel inquired. 'I should be happy to have you join me.'

Her face, I now saw, was enormously kind.

'Didn't he mention inviting me?' I asked.

'No. And I'm afraid he won't be home himself,' she said.

The knot in my throat tightened at this information. For a moment I did not believe her. I wanted to search the flat. I was convinced that Brecht was somewhere out of sight, somewhere along the corridor. Hiding from me.

'Look for yourself,' suggested Weigel, understanding exactly what was going through my head.

I shut my eyes. For some reason her understanding was more painful to me than her mockery would have been.

'I know where he is,' she explained, and her serenity astounded me. 'He is with Carola Neher.'

'He must have forgotten,' I said stupidly.

The contrast between my eagerness to arrive on time, with the weight of the Russian dictionary and the typewriter hurting my fingers, made me want to cry. Weigel saw as much.

'Believe me, dear child,' she said, 'I am very sorry for you.'

My distress may seem irrational. To forget so functional a meeting may not seem the most insulting of Brecht's behaviour. Yet something in the event seemed to wake me out of the dream in which I had been living.

I tried to explain as much to Lenya the next day, but she was impatient with me. She was off to Paris and, although she normally took such moves lightly, I could see something was disturbing her. She kept changing her mind about one dress after another. Finally she threw them all over the bed for her maid to pack. All the time I was speaking, I was conscious of her inner turmoil, without understanding it. As I tried to tease out the sense of my own emotions she rounded on me. My subtleties appalled her. She thought them dishonest.

'I can't *talk* to you about it. Why waste your one and only life?' she raged at me. 'We'll all be dead soon.'

Her words called up a bleak coldness under my heart. Death was daily in the streets of the city, an angry casual violence that took the young as soon as the old. I thought of my own death; I could hear the glass breaking, the violence, the pain and then silence. The blackness of it. I had never been given a religious faith that suggested there was an afterlife.

'Why do you live without sex?' she went on, still in a furious voice.

I tried to explain that if I were going to die young, it was love I needed, not sex.

'How old are you now? Twenty-three?' she asked me, staring. 'It's unnatural.'

'It's a question of *friendship*,' I began to explain. 'Brecht and I are comrades, part of the same organization.'

'I won't talk to you about Brecht,' she said finally. 'Or comradeship. I don't have your sympathy with the comrades. Nor does Kurt.'

'Have you and Kurt quarrelled?' I asked nastily, guessing at the reasons behind her evident inner confusion.

'We still agree about this,' she said.

I saw that their recent tiff had hurt her.

'There is a man I want you to meet,' she said. 'Another writer.'

'I don't want to meet anyone.'

A great fatigue filled me at the thought of forming any other relationship. I shall go home from here, I thought, and sleep for fourteen hours at a stretch. It was a mistake to visit Lenya. It was a mistake to see anyone.

'I don't want to belong to anyone else,' I said.

'He is a poet. You will like him,' she said. She looked at me impishly.

'I suppose he is very handsome and rich,' I said resignedly, remembering the last few men Lenya had introduced me to. They leered at me, and paid for my meals, and it seemed altogether irrelevant.

'No,' she said. 'He is poor, ill and badly dressed.' She smiled. 'They say he is a genius, but how can I tell?'

'A genius is the last thing I want,' I said. 'If I found someone who thought I was important, that would be another matter. But in any case I don't want to try again.'

I remember thinking, what's the point, it will always be the same, trying to belong and failing. 'Something will always go wrong,' I said. 'After all, I don't really care.'

She looked at me strangely. 'That's true,' she said. 'Though you don't understand that yet. When you know that, you will be free.'

I let her kiss me then, without the least interest in being petted further. Feeling as much, she sighed, and patted my rump. 'Listen,' she said, 'you could be the most beautiful thing in the world.'

I made a deprecating face.

'It's fatal to be afraid,' she said. 'Be arrogant. It's the only thing people respect.'

Something in what she said must have affected me.

When I met Seryozha later in the week, I didn't think he was a genius, and I liked him very much. He lived near Pragerplatz, a small, friendly square round which many exiled Russians housed themselves. I liked the neighbourhood; the balalaikas, the

92

gypsies, the pancakes, the shashliks for sale on every side. Russian was spoken everywhere. The great division between émigré and Soviet literature had not yet been drawn; people were still coming in and out of Russia; books from Berlin circulated in Moscow; there were books of Soviet poets everywhere. It was a world where people who had left great estates now lived by washing dishes. Ehrenburg could sometimes be found there, especially in the Pragerdiehle café, where émigrés and Communists alike argued passionately late into the night. Seryozha lived in a large, dark, book-filled room; and his lack of practical ability meant that very clearly he had not solved the problem of lighting his own fire. His background was grand enough, but he had come round to understand the Revolution, and though his every instinct was opposed to violence, he spoke now with sympathy for those who had made it. In those days I could not have respected anyone who did not identify himself with the natural side for men of goodwill.

What I liked in Seryozha was that he was clearly a man whose nerves had been stretched beyond endurance. In Moscow he had been the lover of a grand Russian actress, who had left him for another man. I think she had moved to Paris. The lyrics he showed me were simple, unaffected and filled with his own unhappiness; I guessed he was tubercular, but was not repelled by his illness; even his evident weakness and inability to look after himself pleased me. He was gentle and modest. I liked the way I could help him. He needed socks, and I bought them for him. I insisted he wore warm underwear. In return he lent me books, and I stumbled over them, including the poems he lent me of Akhmatova.

'My greatest influence,' he said mournfully.

And the shafts of her lyrics pierced straight to my own heart.

He was older than I, and calmly pessimistic about this world, even as he planned to return to Russia and join in the struggle to improve it.

'Nothing matters much,' he said.

I questioned that indignantly, full of my own youth and energy and my faith in what communism was doing. He listened with approval and doubt mingled together, pleased with my vehemence.

'I think I'm falling in love with you,' he said.

I knew instinctively that I was the kind of girl he had fallen in love with many times before; and I knew too that he was not the kind of man who would arouse me to the same sort of passion. And yet I loved his melancholy and his need. Most of all what I loved was his vision of me as strong and free. I was much less powerful than he imagined, but I offered him comfort, and if he didn't give me much sexual pleasure he gave me something else that I had almost forgotten: a belief that I was essential.

My chance for a confrontation with Brecht did not come that week, or even that month. He was travelling about the world. He may have been in Russia. Or Paris. I received news of him casually from time to time, but I did not see him. I did not feel as unhappy as I expected; precisely, I suppose, because no decision had been announced to Brecht. I was living in a pause of which he knew nothing. Then, one day, there he was sitting in a café I had gone into after a show.

He was looking fatter and coarser, and I was in two minds whether to sit near him, expecting him to look up casually at best, barely acknowledging my existence. Instead he came over at once to where I was sitting and sat next to me.

'Where have you been?' he asked me, taking my hand. His nails were bitten, and there was a rim of dirt under them. A familiar smell of tobacco and sweat rose from him. Far from finding it repulsive, however, I was deeply moved by his physical presence. It was a long time since he had touched me with tenderness.

'Little Frieda,' he said.

The tenderness weakened me in some central piece of myself. Perhaps he suspected my intentions to break with him, and for that reason had chosen to be at his most loving.

'Are you free tonight?' he asked me.

'I'm afraid not,' I said.

'You are angry with me,' he said reproachfully.

I stared at him with as much hostility as I could muster.

'You look like a child today. I adore you when you look like that,' he said to me. 'We must renew our pact of friendship.' The word 'friendship', with all its connotations of trust and working side by side, aroused even more powerfully the emotions I hoped to lose.

'We arranged to work on translations one night last month,' I said. 'At your flat. I suppose that dropped out of your mind?'

He sighed. 'Do you know what is happening in the world around us? Are you going to punish me for so little?'

I drew in a deep breath. 'You shouldn't pretend to love me,' I said. 'When you don't. It isn't fair.'

His eyebrows shot up at the note in my voice. 'I've never pretended anything,' he said. 'To anyone. Have I ever pretended?'

'I don't care about your kind of honesty,' I said. 'It's just a way of doing whatever you want without promising anything. I've had enough of all that.'

He must have been surprised, but his face, which had been warm and loving until that moment, suddenly took on an ironic expression. 'Have you?'

'Because I know I don't matter to you,' I said, less assertively.

'We can't discuss these things here,' he said, frowning.

'Why not let me go? You have enough helpers. You won't notice,' I said.

I made to rise, but he put his hand on my arm to prevent me. 'I see,' he said. 'You are being unfaithful to me.'

I could feel the colour coming up, not only in my cheeks but all over my face and neck. 'What does it matter if I am?' I said weakly.

I tried to call up the feeling of Seryozha's warm soft kiss, and his nervy body against mine.

'Will you leave the company?' asked Brecht.

'I don't know yet.'

'You must be very confident of your talents,' he said, his eyes searching my face with a certain malice.

My heart was beginning to bang a little, for reasons I did not yet understand.

'Yes,' he said. 'Very courageous.' He patted my hand and smiled. 'Only the real originals of this world can afford to stand alone.'

I lifted my chin a little tremulously.

'Perhaps you are even thinking of leaving Berlin?' he asked.

'Everyone is,' I said.

'You should not risk America,' he said. 'You know that, don't you?'

'Why not?'

'The Americans look for something in the theatre which you do not have. Remember that. I know about these things. Paris?' He seemed to consider for a moment. Then he shook his head. 'I don't think you could manage it. Do you?'

'I have been invited for a fortnight to Moscow,' I said hesitantly.

'A fortnight's work?' In his mouth it seemed a poor opportunity, almost a declaration of Russian reluctance to commit themselves longer. 'Surprising,' he said. 'When they are so desperate for comrades from other countries.'

'I shall *make* them like me,' I said, lifting my chin defiantly.

'Yes?' His voice rose sceptically. 'You are not Lenya, you know.'

I agreed I was not.

'It is not a question of stage presence,' he warned me. 'I don't deny once you are on a stage people look and listen with interest. But offstage, you are too timid and shy, aren't you, my little Frieda? You have nothing to say to people. And you will need that.'

His words entered under my ribs and spiked my trembling heart.

'I only say these things for your own good,' he soothed me. 'Encouragement isn't always sensible. It can only help to know the truth.'

I wanted to claim something for myself, but I could not. 'Is Berlin so different, then?' I managed to whisper.

He laughed at me. 'Do you imagine you have made your own work here? You *are* ungrateful. Don't you see, you have worked as part of a team?'

'I work on my own in cabaret,' I said truculently.

Even as I said as much I knew it was not altogether so, that most of my opportunities had come from the endeavour we had shared.

'You talk nonsense sometimes, don't you?' he teased me. 'Can you let yourself know that? I made you, Frieda. You be careful of thinking you can exist without me.'

96

I stood up then, even though my limbs were shaking. It was dangerous to let any more of his words enter me. I should lose all faith in myself. I tried to remember what Lenya had said to me. It was gone. I stood there trembling with his vision of my being running round in my blood like a poison.

He looked at me thoughtfully. 'Is he a good lover, this new man of yours?' he asked.

I could think of nothing to say about that. I had forgotten Seryozha altogether.

'Women have to put up with things,' he said. 'You will find it is not so different with him, in the upshot.'

I strode out of the room.

And then the pain began. I wanted to fall out of love with Brecht. Instead I fell out of love with myself. And for all Seryozha's sweetness, his love and need were not enough to make me self-confident. He saw as much, as if he expected it.

I went on working as best I could, though cabarets were closing. The police did nothing to prevent incursions of Nazi violence into them. Early in 1932 I had to stop for another reason. I discovered I was having a child. I was already six months' pregnant when I went to the doctor to find reasons for my recent fainting. As soon as I was told that I was bearing a child, I began to stand like a pregnant woman, and cabaret work was out of the question. I was not altogether sorry. I could feel the child jumping under my skin when I lay in bed. Seryozha put his hand to the skin and rejoiced; I hoped it was his child.

We lived for a time on my savings. But it was not uncommon for people, poor in every part of their own lives, to have friends who could offer them a holiday from poverty. And a friend of Seryozha had a château near Juan-les-Pins. Soon after I stopped work in Berlin, a letter came with just such an invitation for us.

I was in an unfamiliar, languorous state; the physiology of my condition induced its own tranquillity. I had enough money to buy the train tickets. Seryozha had the invitation. So it was we went to stay with the Skrebensky family. We shared a white bedroom with its own bathroom; in the morning everyone swam

97

in the blue sea. Seryozha wrote his poems; I improved my Russian. We forgot after a few days everything that was happening in Germany. Indeed, in some sense those horrors were never as real to Seryozha as to me, because all his sense of loss was attached to Russia.

In the house by the sea, we ate good French food. But the Skrebenskys talked of nothing but Russia: about when they could return there, and the terrible homesickness they all experienced; the enormity of the soul of the country and the lure of its snow and forests. Seryozha argued with them that return was possible, and sometimes I joined in, using my poor spoken Russian as best I could to assert we were all needed in the New Society. I don't think they paid much attention. The Skrebenskys had been in Russia through the civil war, they spoke of people burning books in order to heat one room during the famine; Skrebensky himself had been in the Crimea and spoke of eating dogs.

I went to bed much earlier than Seryozha. The others were drunk in a civilized, beautiful way every night. I drank little, since I was close to giving birth to my daughter. Sometimes I was mildly happy. I got very brown. I relaxed. Sometimes the family went to Monte Carlo to gamble; Seryozha went too. And I didn't mind being left alone. I read; devoured books of poetry. It was the most sustained patch of reading in my entire life. I learnt the poems I liked by heart and said them to Seryozha in the mornings. He lay in bed much later than I did, sleepily listening to me, and correcting my uncertain pronunciation.

Sometimes, when they were all out playing cards and I was alone except for the servants, I looked out of the window at the sea and the light was inexpressibly sad. Then the poems I read only increased the sadness. I hardly dared to read Brecht's poetry.

'I don't know if I could ever be a Communist,' Seryozha said when I expressed my enthusiasm for visiting his country for that reason. 'I'm not sure at all.'

I wheedled and argued for the inevitability of socialism. 'Everything is coming out as Marx said. Look what is happening all over Europe.'

'I don't know what sense to make of it,' he said. 'Are you sure?

To go back to Russia would make me very happy. Do you think they will overlook my lack of political commitment?'

'Of course,' I said. It was quite beyond me to imagine that the country of socialism would be anything but fair.

So it was, even before Hitler came to power, and thinking less of danger than excitement and opportunity, we made our plans to return to Russia as soon as the baby was born and strong enough to travel.

We were like children. Like orphans.

I had arranged to give birth to my child in Berlin; I don't think in advance I worried much about doing so; I did not expect to die then. Nor did I expect to suffer as much as I did. It was a difficult birth, so difficult that I made a vow never to endure such pain again. It did not prevent me instantly loving my daughter. I can still smell the sweetness of her clean hair and feel her eager lips on my breast. When they brought her to me the first time, I saw her perfection at once. She looked a little like that photograph of Minna that had stood upon the piano long ago in the house where I had once lived with my own mother and father. She had a great deal of fair hair, and a neat small nose. Only her eyes, I saw, were rounder and darker and more like mine. As her small fingers twitched, I examined their delicacy with astonishment; soon I was happily kissing the softness of her tender little feet.

We had returned to a small flat, which made it difficult to cope. The soiled napkins had to be boiled, and the kitchen was small; three people made what had once seemed luxurious to me something less than comfortable; Seryozha went out during the day to get away, and I found the effort of keeping the rooms even moderately clean was too much for me. But I did not feel miserable about that. The room was just a staging post; as soon as the child was a year or two older we would be setting off for Russia.

In retrospect my complacency in those last months in Berlin, cleaning my daughter and watching her fatten, crawl and take steps from my hand to Seryozha's, is hard to explain. 1932, a brutal year, hardly reached us. We knew there were seven million unemployed, that people were hungry. Yet the Kufürstendamm was still ablaze with lights. The shop windows still displayed the most luxurious goods. If we bought little, it still seemed to be our choice, just as we lived simply, with little interest in expensive restaurants.

In the northern part of the city, the winter made itself felt; the cold winds blew from the Baltic and found the homeless looking for a dosshouse. They could not always afford even that. A bunk in a dosshouse cost fifty pfennigs, and the dole was nine marks a month. There were always people with wide eyes looking into the huge window of a snack bar near Alexanderplatz which offered potatoes with bacon and sausages.

Once an old woman ran past me as I pushed my daughter back home. She was sobbing loudly. It was already dark; a December evening, with the smell of coal fires in the damp air and a wind getting in under my coat. I heard a shot ring out nearby and there was a scuffle of men running away, and then the police. The Nazis had shot a Communist worker in the street.

All these horrors I endured calmly. I even remember listening to an old journalist friend of mine explaining that weak legs was a true sign of Jewish ancestry and feeling more disgust than terror. We were going to leave in our own good time and for our own reasons. I still had a little money. We had put aside the train fare for Russia.

Then the Nazis won the elections.

3

It won't last, people said. Germany is good. This is the country of Heine and Beethoven. The country of Schiller. It will not tolerate the rule of uniformed thugs. I wondered what Brecht and Hauptmann, whom I had hardly seen since I came back to Berlin, were thinking about Hitler's triumph.

Early in May I telephoned Bess Hauptmann one morning from a public box while Seryozha slept. She had heard of my pregnancy; she asked about the child; she also asked if I had seen Brecht recently.

'No,' I said.

'He is in hospital,' she said.

A ripple of distrust went through me. He had often been hypochondriac about his heart; it had been a useful excuse which had once prevented him from entering the army in the First World War; he was always afraid it would explode.

'I'd like to see *you*,' I said firmly. 'Not Brecht. I want to discuss what is best to do.'

She invited me to see her that evening.

'Be careful,' she warned me.

I left the baby with Seryozha.

Bess opened the door to me on a chain, as if fearing who might be standing there.

'They took two people from next door,' she explained. 'Last night.'

She was wearing a huge overcoat, and was shaking with what looked like extreme cold. When we went in, I saw she had been drinking brandy; she poured me a glass, which I waved away.

'Are you all right?' I asked.

For answer she got to her feet, and ran from the room. Presently I could hear her retching in the bathroom. When she came back, she was wearing no make-up, and there was sweat on her forehead and cheeks.

'You're ill,' I said, concerned.

The place was bare, like a cell. She shook her head, still shaking feverishly. 'I can still see it,' she said. 'They dropped him from the window. He was only nineteen.'

I gathered she was talking about the people from next door.

'Why?' I asked. 'There must have been a reason.'

'I didn't even know them,' she said.

I was aware of her trembling, and could say nothing.

'It's so arbitrary. They called me in a week or so ago, and let me go without much trouble. They took in Helli Weigel . . .'

'What happened to her?' I asked quickly, remembering she was Jewish.

'They let her go. Well, have you made your arrangements?'

'I've made a decision,' I said. 'What about you?'

She shook her head. 'I can't leave,' she said. 'There's too much to be done.'

'And Brecht? What are his plans?' I spoke without the least wavering in my voice.

'Weigel will look after things,' she said.

'Is Lenya still in Paris?' I asked.

Bess's lips curled a little, not exactly with contempt but with a dislike of those whose pleasures were so different from her own. 'She will fall on her feet,' she said. 'Her life will be extravagant, luxurious. Bath salts. Scents. Crystal bottles. Like walking into a movie.'

There was a part of me that resonated with envy at the thought of such pleasures. 'Seryozha and I are going to Russia,' I said, with a certain pride.

Before leaving, I thought I should say goodbye to my father. I planned to leave him a little money. I sent him a note; half wondering if he would reply. His handwriting on the scribbled note he returned gave me a little jolt. He was lonely now, he said, and was eager to see me.

I arrived at the same flat late one evening, after putting my daughter to sleep in her cot; perhaps I should have brought her to

102

see him, but something prevented me from making that gesture of forgiveness.

He opened the door to me, sober and cleanly dressed, and I was touched to smell the odours of an old-fashioned chicken soup. The effort that he had put into it showed itself in the untidiness of the kitchen and his intent expression as he put the bowl before me. For a moment I wanted to cry.

'Eat, my child,' he said, almost as though nothing had ever been wrong between us.

I ate as well as I could.

'It is dangerous here for Jews,' I said.

He shrugged. 'What can they do to me? Kill me? I'll be dead soon anyway.' His eyes brooded over my face. 'What can they do to me?' he asked again. 'What could be worse than the way I live now?'

'They may not let you make good chicken soup,' I suggested.

'I don't care what I eat,' he said. 'My life is over. When your mother died it was all over for me.'

It was a remark that so astonished me I was tempted for a moment to argue resentfully, remembering my poor hard-working mother.

'You seem to be managing very well without her,' I said.

'I am already dead,' he said.

Something in his face prevented me from accusing him of melodrama and I went over, took his hands and wished him well. Both of us wept.

I ran into Weigel in the street the following day, and she seemed for a moment hardly to recognize me. Then she seized my arm and issued a warning.

'Don't hesitate,' she said without being more precise.

There was no one near us, outside on the street; there was a wind blowing; yet we both spoke in low voices.

'Brecht is in hospital,' she said.

It was as if she was giving me permission to go and see him, and this time I did not deny my interest.

'Give me the address,' I asked simply.

It was the last goodbye I would make.

That night several members of the Communist Party were picked up and taken away. Weigel was lucky; she had been staying with friends when they went to the flat, and Brecht was safe in his clinic room. The news had reached Brecht before I did, and he was for that reason more grumpy and anxious than pleased to see me. But when I came and sat next to his bed he took both my hands and looked into my eyes.

'Dark times,' he said. 'People who come after us will judge us badly. At least let's forgive one another.'

I nodded my willingness.

'I am as unhappy as you are,' he said.

Tears came to my eyes as he said so. I had not seen him for so long and had tried so hard not to think of him.

'It's not your fault,' he said. 'Nor mine. What we feel for each other.' He was gripping my wrists so hard that it hurt me, but I didn't care. I knew he was talking about far more than his treatment of me. 'Just accept it,' he said. 'Don't strain against it. That's how things are.'

'Are you leaving Berlin?' I asked.

'People say things aren't going to get better for a long time.'

'I shall go to Russia,' I said.

He looked at me darkly. 'And the child?

'I didn't know you knew about the child,' I stammered.

'Is it mine?' he asked.

'I don't think so,' I said.

He nodded. 'You will all be safer there,' he said.

I believed it. Russia would be my family; larger, stronger and more able to protect me than an ordinary family; I thought of it as home, as the Brecht workshop had been home for me.

'I suppose you will go there too?' I asked. 'When you can.' I could see that he had not yet accepted the idea of leaving Germany.

'I don't know what we will do,' he said.

Is it only hindsight that makes me remember a kind of craftiness in his smile as he said those words? There was always something ambiguous in his grin. When I left him, it was not the pressure of his hands or the forgiving words we exchanged I remembered, but a glitter of black eyes behind tin glasses and that grin. That very night, telling no one, he and Weigel and the children left for Vienna.

Seryozha knew at once that I had seen Brecht again. I admitted as much, even while denying there was any feeling left between us. My protests affected Seryozha badly.

'I have lost many women,' he said, 'but I have never shared them.'

His assumptions angered me and when he tried to take me in his arms that anger made me stiffen. He felt my reluctance and looked even sadder. 'You don't love me any more,' he said.

'Let's just be kind to one another,' I said. 'Please?'

He looked at the marks on my arm where Brecht had gripped my wrist, and frowned, while I looked at him with pity and impatience.

'I see I can no longer trust you about anything,' he said.

I shrugged.

Later, when we were friendlier, he explained he was edgy because he had arranged for us to go to Russia earlier than we had planned and he already felt guilty about how I would manage with the baby. I reassured him that I should manage well enough. So it was I went into exile.

PART FOUR

MOSCOW

'For the waterwheel must keep on turning
And so what's on top is bound to fall.
All the time the water underneath is learning
It has to drive the water wheel.'

Brecht: 'Ballad of the Waterwheel'

1

The journey to Moscow by train is long; the child was fretful; and we sat up tending her in turns. In the daylight hours those miles of Russian space seemed flat and forbidding. Whenever my eyes closed in sleep, I dreamed of large, unfamiliar faces hovering above me, and kept waking with a terrified jerk. Fortunately, when we were still about a hundred kilometres from Moscow, two friends from Berlin – for many of us ran East – put their heads round the door. Laughing and a little drunk, they began to talk excitedly of Moscow theatre, Meierhold, and Chinese dancers, and passed round a silver flask of vodka, which Seryozha gulped down gratefully.

I could see he was anxious, even though our passports were in order and I knew he had made arrangements to work as a translator. For my part, I felt confused and lonely. As I rocked the child, I consoled myself with the thought of the brilliance of the Moscow we were going towards.

It is hard to focus on a completely unfamiliar scene. When we arrived at Moscow station, the bustle of people, their strange dress, the half-understood tongues all bewildered me. Our Berlin friends were swept away. There were only shabby and unknown people around us. I was clutching the child to me, with my heart dropping, when a thin-faced young man came up to us.

He had been deputed to help Seryozha, he said; we had been given a flat; I need not worry. There were a great many Germans from the Berlin theatre in Moscow, and they remembered me. His courtesy to me was particularly marked.

We had been placed out in the suburbs of the city. The snows were piled twenty feet high on each side of the road. It may have been the excitement, but I did not feel the cold. The air was bright and dry, and Seryozha's friend had brought me a fur hat. This was important, he said, since so much body heat is lost through the

109

head. I tucked the hat round my daughter's head, and wrapped her even more closely in her shawl.

The block which we had been allocated was poor, even by the most impoverished German standards, and we had to walk up the stone stairs to the fifth floor because the lift was not working. I could smell something familiar and ugly. When we turned on to our own landing I recognised it as the smell of stale urine. Our flat was one room only, with a gas stove in a corner. Before this could depress us, however, the tenants of the neighbouring flats came in to welcome us. There were people of all ages, all Russian, and they brought vodka which we drank out of thick china, laughing as we did so. Soon there were tins of sardines and black bread; someone gave the child hard candy. That first night's welcome was more than I had expected; in my fatigue I was ready to cry with happiness at so much hugging, so many eager people. For the first time our escape into a new world seemed an unmitigated good fortune.

The gas had not yet been connected, we found the next morning; and I had to cook food for the child on a kerosene stove in the corridor. We remained cheerful. The cooker in the flat was to be ready soon, we were told; and a neighbour lent us an oilcloth to throw over the stove so that it could be used as a table.

Seryozha had an appointment for lunch at the Writers' House; and I went too, to see what arrangements could be made for myself. The same thin-faced gentleman escorted us to our rendezvous. The Dom Literaterov, the home of the Writers' Union, is housed in what was once the Solugub mansion, that house which Tolstoy described as belonging to the family Rostov. It was still grand, though shabby, as we walked up its staircases, admired its chandeliers, and were taken into its restaurant.

This was a large room with balconies ornately carved in dark wood. There were silver dishes, in which lay mushrooms or liver, and from which rose a delicious aroma of herbs and garlic. To eat in such a restaurant was a great privilege, and the writers present were celebrating suitably. There were a great many bottles of champagne.

'Sovietskaya champagne,' our guide pointed out proudly.

We sat under the carved wooden balconies, and were offered

110

sour plums and pickled tomatoes. No one objected to our daughter sitting at our side, and eating her own minute mouthfuls.

'It's like fairyland,' I said.

'Look,' said Seryozha, 'I recognize that face.'

It might have been Babel. Or Petrov.

I sat and waited for Seryozha to come out of his interview with one of the underlings of the translators' publishing house, idly watching to see who else could be recognized. There was indeed a strong German contingent. I caught a glimpse of someone who looked like Carola Neher, as beautiful as ever, but blonder and plumper.

When Seryozha came back he was frowning.

'They want to see you,' he said.

'I can't work as a translator,' I said, startled.

'I know,' he said.

We were both puzzled.

Behind the desk sat a woman with a solid peasant face.

'Of course we know who you are,' she said, with a brilliant smile.

I didn't think I had international fame, and said so.

'Perhaps not,' she smiled, 'but you were connected to Brecht for many years, isn't that so?'

'No longer,' I said firmly.

'But you worked together?'

'I was in several of his plays,' I agreed. And I thought to myself, well, why not take some advantage from that?

'Exactly,' she said, nodding. 'Part of his group.'

I agreed that was so.

'When did you last see him?' she asked me with a frankness that removed all my suspicions.

'In hospital,' I told her.

'Do you know where he is now?'

'No,' I said. It was true.

'Denmark. His wife is coming here.' She consulted notes on her desk. 'For a reading tour. I think they will find things hard in the capitalist West with his convictions, don't you?'

'Brecht has many admirers,' I said.

111

'His money will be blocked by the Nazis, however,' she said. 'He may need help. And surely the whole family would be better here?'

I agreed warmly that this was so, and she looked pleased.

'Is your flat comfortable?' she asked.

I hesitated, and then mentioned the problems with the gas stove, and the plywood chair that cracked under me when I tried to lift the cases above the wardrobe. She had not expected my story, and she looked discomfited.

'We will move you closer to the centre,' she said. 'It's an error.'

'Could you,' I wondered, 'find me some work? I have an introduction to the Meierhold Theatre, but I don't think my Russian is good enough to do anything but sing and dance.'

'We'll find you something,' she said. 'If we can.'

I gasped. It all seemed too good to be true.

We walked around the Arbat Square and along Nikita Boulevard, making out the names of movie theatres. The Arbat Art, the Carnival and the Prague. We got as far as Pushkin's monument. 'Let's sit,' I said.

Seryozha swept the snow away, and we sat down side by side.

'I think we are going to be happy here,' I said.

2

The flat we moved to had three rooms. It was in central Moscow, near Lavrushinsky; the rooms were larger and taller, and though the furniture was shabby, it had once been good.

Seryozha worked on translations of Byelorussian and Ukrainian poets; he grumbled a little at having to work from literal versions of poems in languages he did not know, rather than use his excellent French and German, but he seemed happy enough. We began to meet our neighbours, more soberly than we had in our first apartment. Most of them were literary in one way or another, we discovered.

Among them, I recognized a girl from Berlin. She had delicate, bony features, the kind that photograph well but often look drawn and pale. I recognized her from Aufricht's theatre. She had been acting in *Mother* while I was upstairs in the chorus line of *Mahagonny*. It was Grete Steffin, another of Brecht's girls, I remembered; but that was no concern of mine now. We smiled and exchanged a few words in German. Her smile lit her face, but she looked ill much of the time. One day she stopped and seemed to feel towards a memory of her own.

'Aren't you Frieda Bloom?' she asked me. 'I heard you sing once at Westerborg's café.'

I agreed I was, but it seemed such another world from the one in which we now found ourselves that my acknowledgement was only rueful, and I pushed the acquaintance no further.

One day, when Seryozha was at the library, I found I had no matches to light the stove, knocked on her door, and was asked into her flat for coffee. She was looking particularly frail, and for the first time I listened to her tearing cough and guessed she was tubercular.

'Yes,' she admitted, when I asked her whether she had been treated. 'In the Crimea. When I first came here there was a hole in my lungs the size of an egg but it's better now.'

I doubted whether she was completely cured for all her lightness of tone. I could see that she took inadequate care of her cough. And I could not help speculating what there was to attract Brecht to such a woman. Everything about her was pointed; her cheekbones, her facial shape, her delicate wrists; her thinness, which made me feel gross in comparison. Yet for all her fragility, there was the toughness of someone who worked enormously hard; when I passed her room, even in the middle of the night, I could see the line of light under her door and hear the tap of her typewriter keys. When the cold made me complain that I missed my flat in Berlin, she dismissed my words.

'It doesn't matter what our conditions are like,' she said. Without saying any more she made me see her as a soldier, as someone in the fight for a great cause. And in her flash of contempt for what she recognized in my voice, I understood what Brecht loved in her. It was what she could do without; she had an inner core that made it possible for her to survive in almost any conditions; she was indomitable because she could carry on without comfort. The Communist ideology endorsed that pride; it was natural that she should be so fanatically attached to the Party. In her, Brecht loved the proletariat itself.

I refused to be cowed by her moral intensity, however. I smiled instead and she had the grace to join me. As she did so, I felt a great wave of pity for her. She might drop dead, I saw suddenly, from an undernourishment she hardly noticed.

'I confess I was always more sybaritic,' I said. 'I miss soft pillows and satin sheets.'

'Do you get the news from Germany?' she asked me, generously giving me credit for more serious emotions.

'There have been killings and arrests,' I said sombrely.

'Worse,' she said. 'The defeat is almost complete.'

'Russia is the only hope,' I said.

A look I could not altogether read crossed her face. 'We must hope so,' she said.

'I believe Brecht is in Denmark,' I said, feeling for information about him as fingers investigate a sore place, tentatively but with pleasure.

'We have been working on some interesting plays,' she said energetically.

I remembered now that she, like Bess, worked alongside him as a writer sometimes. A ripple of jealousy, the first I had felt in her presence, ruffled my inner composure.

'Where is Bess Hauptmann?' I asked.

'She is still in Germany,' she said. 'Trying to get as many of his manuscripts out as possible.'

'And Helli Weigel?'

'It is hard for her to find proper work. She can only speak German,' said Grete.

There I was sympathetic. The problem with anything like proper work for me was my Russian. I could just about read and write, but no one wanted to use me on the stage. The warmth and friendliness of that first interview at the Writers' House had led nowhere. So I was turned into a consumer. For a time I enjoyed this well enough, because for all the grubbiness of the theatres, the productions were still at their most adventurous.

One day, when *Hamlet* was playing at the Vakhtangov Theatre, with the fat little actor Goryunov in the lead, I was standing waiting for a drink when I recognized the woman from the Writers' Union who had found us our flat. She was arguing with the young man behind the table.

'I only drink Georgian Borzhomi mineral water,' she was saying.

I tapped her on the shoulder, and she looked round, startled.

After a moment she recognized me.

'I still need help finding a job,' I said boldly. 'Can you do anything?'

She hesitated. 'Wait for a week or so,' she said doubtfully. 'I don't know. The man you need to see is busy. I will arrange an appointment with someone in the theatre section. Perhaps they will find something.'

I was a little lowered by this response as I made my way back to Seryozha, but I was stopped before I could reach him by a smartly dressed middle-aged woman who spoke German with an

American accent. 'I saw you in Berlin,' she said. 'Aren't you Frieda Bloom?'

I agreed wanly that I was.

'Well, for heaven's sake. Everyone is here,' she said. 'Isn't it the most exciting place for theatre in the whole world?'

I agreed it might well be but I was too dispirited by my inconclusive encounter with the union official to sound enthusiastic.

She paused and looked at me closely. 'I hear rumours from time to time,' she frowned.

I hastened to explain that my reservations were not political.

'Do you find work?' she asked.

I admitted that was difficult.

At that she paused. 'They are all right with Jews here, aren't they? I've been asking about that, and it's not a problem here, is it?'

'No,' I said.

Someone at my side began to laugh.

'Come to the States,' she suggested. 'It is a country of immigrants. I can get you a visa.'

'Do people play my records there?' I asked.

'I don't know,' she confessed, and mumbled something about Lenya in Paris. 'Learn English,' she advised me.

'I knew some as a child,' I said doubtfully. My experience with Russian had not given me great confidence in my linguistic skills.

'Well, I'm going off on a plane tomorrow. I would have so liked to talk more to you.'

'I expect we'll meet again,' I said, without much interest.

There were few books that taught English, and when Seryozha found me poring over one he began to show the same anger that he had expressed when he found me writing songs in German.

'The less one writes the better,' he muttered.

'But you are a writer,' I exclaimed.

'A translator is safe enough,' he said. 'And even then we can be unlucky.'

He wanted to be happy in his country, he liked to be speaking his own language again, but I could see he was uneasy. 'I hear

116

more than you do, locked away here in your cocoon with the baby,' he said.

'Do you think I like that? I'm bored out of my mind,' I flared.

The colour was high in his face, and his eyes were pink with emotions I could not read.

'Kirov is dead,' he said.

It meant nothing to me.

He told me there had been an assassination, that there were plots, mass arrests. 'Purges,' he said.

It was the first time I had heard the word.

'We must be careful,' he warned me.

'What do you think? They are looking for traitors among people like us?' I mocked him.

'You are a foreigner,' he pointed out. 'They might well suspect you.'

'And your family fought on the wrong side,' I pointed out sulkily.

He went very quiet.

'Do you think I don't remember that,' he said after a time.

One day Seryozha came home from work worried because there was sabotage at the office.

'How?' I asked, amused.

'Files burnt. Books destroyed. Worse . . .'

He had brought in a bottle of vodka, and he took it out of his pocket then with an inelegant movement, and drank from the neck of the bottle. When he saw me looking at that gesture, he wiped his lips shamefacedly. Then he began to tell me about a meeting of the Translators' Union in his office, and the way they had argued about one of their fellow workers who was taken away. I repeated his words stupidly.

'What was she arrested for?' I asked.

'They say she was a smuggler,' he said hesitantly.

'Well then,' I consoled him, sensing his anxiety.

'I always thought she was a bit fishy,' he muttered.

And then in an unusual excess of passion, he seized me and pulled up my skirt as I sat on the sofa.

Afterwards he fell asleep, and I went to wash away the traces of a passion I had not shared.

Altogether I was not very happy; I missed everything that had made me feel alive. I no longer enjoyed making love; I had forgotten what it was like to step out before the footlights and feel the electricity of an audience's attention upon me. I was doing less and less every day. I tried to make friends with other neighbours apart from Steffin, who had gone back to Denmark. Among these was a large-boned, handsome woman, whose rat-faced husband was working for the Bolshoi as a stage designer. Her name was Olga. She smoked continuously, laughed at my Russian, and taught me to drink vodka. Nothing seemed to discomfit her; she could make a marvellous soup from a handful of potatoes and a knob of garlic. Only once did I see her alarmed. She had been grumbling about her husband's sexual neglect, and I risked an obscene joke, to which she reacted awkwardly. I realized that what had been commonplace in Berlin was a serious matter in Moscow.

'The Nazis hate homosexuals too,' I reflected thoughtlessly, and her broad face looked even more alarmed. 'A different matter, of course,' I said hastily.

3

It was like becoming a ghost.

When the invitation came, I had begun to put on weight through too much potato soup and nightly drinking. It was an invitation to a party at the flat of a notable member of the inner circle of the Writers' Union. There was to be a party for visiting notables of the German émigré community, and I was invited to sing at it.

The thought was like a charge of adrenalin to every cell in my body. In one moment I remembered I was alive. But I was terrified too. Should I sing in German? Or would it be sensible to translate some of the songs into Russian? I called in Seryozha to help me.

'What should I wear?' I asked him.

'How can it matter?' he asked sullenly.

I stopped eating. In the three weeks before the party I was close enough to my former shape to get into a shimmering green dress from my Berlin days.

I looked at myself in the mirror, combed my hair and remembered. I was still Frieda Bloom.

It must have been about this time that I heard Brecht was coming to Moscow. He and some of his entourage were coming on a visit to the Soviet Union. They would be at the party. I would be singing in their honour.

The news came to me from Steffin who had come back from Denmark looking even thinner and iller than in the months before her departure. She knocked on my door on her return and I followed her into her flat, eager for gossip.

'I'm freezing cold,' she said, and she looked as if she had a temperature. 'I am trying to get the *Threepenny Novel* through the Soviet bureaucracy,' she explained, and I guessed that most of the work on that book was hers.

'How is Brecht?' I asked in as neutral a tone as I could muster.

She shook her head. 'You can't imagine how difficult life is for him. He runs round the world. Paris. New York. The work he wants to do simply can't be done any more.'

'Is he short of money?' I asked sceptically.

'It's hard to live as a refugee,' she said. 'He has some money due from royalties over here. And some of his old friends here, like Piscator, could give him work. What do you think?'

I agreed he might be better off in Moscow.

My feelings were now confused. The resurgence of life I had experienced at the prospect of working, even if only for an evening, was now disturbed by the thought of encountering Brecht again. The prospect filled me with resentment. I recognized the shape without surprise. Brecht would be as he always was, at the centre of attention, and the rest of us would have to be satisfied with offering our efforts for his approval. No doubt he had earned the right to sit at the centre of his own life, I thought, but we all have a life and I wanted to sit at the centre of my own.

Either the work, or the thought of seeing Brecht, would have acted as a tonic on their own. The two excitements together agitated me.

There were soon other matters to trouble me. The following night Seryozha and I came back from visiting one of his friends. As soon as we came into the flat, I was aware of something strange. But what was it? Everything looked much as it had before we went out. Not altogether though. In a rare burst of tidiness I had taken away the ashtrays that Seryozha filled with his cigarettes, and washed them along with the tea things. Now they were filled once again with ash.

'Who has been here?' I asked.

We both knew it could only be the secret police.

'I have nothing to hide,' Seryozha said, frowning, but he looked worried.

4

I needed to rehearse with a pianist, and Steffin suggested someone who had once played the piano for the Yiddish theatre, Itzik from Odessa who wore a trilby hat on his head even indoors, and spoke bad German. Itzik laughed at everything, even disasters, and when his parents had difficulties getting permission to come to Moscow, he even mocked their Party cards. 'Times were bad, nobody wanted us, but they believed things were going to be better,' he explained. 'That's why they're called revolutionaries.' He had the licence of a clown, at least in those days. I liked him instantly, and he liked me, or more exactly, he liked the person I became when I sang, which was quite different from the one Seryozha saw every day.

I was not kind to Seryozha. I flared with rage at his smallest criticism; screamed at him when he looked through the piles of washing for the socks I had once delighted to provide. Now I turned all the resentment I felt at my life in the Moscow suburbs on him, as if he had persuaded me to come to Russia against my will. The alleviation of the monotony with Itzik only made me fouler-tempered when I returned.

I tried to explain my ill-behaviour to Steffin one night, holding the child in my arms because a new tooth made her fretful.

'Seryozha is too gentle. Women like us respond better to brutes,' she said.

'Like us?' I queried, wandering across to her work table. She turned away from the sink with a glass in her hand, and grimaced as she swallowed two large tablets. 'My last,' she said of the pills, and coughed. She was wearing a thick overcoat, and a woollen hat pulled over her ears for warmth which made her peaky little face look comic. I offered her some sleeping pills.

'I only need four hours sleep a night,' she said, 'but my ear is very painful. Do you think they would help?'

I looked at her wan face and saw her eyes were clouded with fever. 'What does the doctor say?' I asked.

She hesitated, then confessed. 'It may be tubercular.'

'You should look after yourself,' I reproached her.

I saw now she was limping a little as she brought the kettle to the table to make some tea; and guessed her knee, which had given her some trouble, was swollen again. 'You should be in hospital,' I said.

'There's too much work for that,' she replied.

Her resignation filled me with anger. I could not find her reckless indifference to suffering admirable, even if it was the stuff of martyrs and saints. I tried to say as much, taking her hand, but she pulled away jerkily.

'I won't live long anyway,' she said, almost as if she had seen her death in my eyes. 'I went to a fortune-teller in Germany, long ago. And it's not important to me.' She smiled impishly then as if the superstition were a luxury she could permit herself just because of her stern beliefs.

Rebuffed, I stared down at the table, recognizing pages of Brecht's handwriting, and remembering she had grouped us together as women who liked to sacrifice ourselves. She had found out about my relationship with Brecht long ago; but I hated her assumption that I was still bound to him as she was. My anger made me cruel.

'Does he still write to you?' I asked.

'He sends me poems,' she said, shivering a little although the room was not cold.

'Poor Grete,' I said. 'If you went south, as you should, would Brecht go out of his way to see you?'

She flushed. 'Sometimes I'm sorry for myself,' she said, shrugging. 'But you know Brecht. I accept him. And we still have good times together.'

'You do so much for him. Do you really suppose he values it?' I said, gesturing at the manuscripts on the table.

She smiled and I knew I had put it wrongly, that Brecht certainly found her work valuable, and that she knew as much. It wasn't what I meant to be saying. 'He doesn't care for anyone but himself,' I said.

'And that is fine,' she said with spirit. 'I don't want to be cared for or taken care of. It's not important to me.'

'What is important to you?'

'Look at this,' she suggested. She showed me a draft copy of what I now know to be *The Good Woman of Setzuan* in her own handwriting.

'Is this his?' I asked.

'Not yet,' she said.

The child had fallen asleep on my shoulder. I risked putting her down on the coverlet of the bed, though I kept my hand on her back warmly. The child stirred a little, but remained asleep while I read. It was not yet the complete play, just a few scenes, but I recognized at once that Steffin had an extraordinary talent. I don't mean the concepts were original. The idea that goodness has to compromise with evil to survive was altogether Brecht's but there was something of her own, something poignant in the character of the central girl which was new to me. I recognized a wish for goodness and simplicity, and a despair in finding either.

'A sad tale,' I said.

She shrugged. 'The world is as it is.'

'What else have you written?' I asked her.

For answer she gave me a handful of scribbled pages, and I read them hungrily. She had caught Brecht's style just as I had once tried to do. Yet the lyrics were fresh and pungent. Later in life I read one or two of those very poems attributed to Brecht in a German collection but I had no doubt either that night or later that Steffin had written them herself.

'Has Brecht seen these?' I asked.

She smiled. 'I send them to him.'

'They are very fine,' I said.

'I am only a beginner,' she said.

'These are more than beginning,' I exclaimed. 'What does he say of these?'

'I don't like to worry him with my need for an opinion,' she said, frowning. 'It makes me feel guilty whenever I do it.'

123

'You idiot,' I shouted, so that the child woke, and I had to take her back in my arms, and walk about the room again, patting her vigorously. 'You have a true talent. Something real that belongs to you. Don't let him steal it.'

'It's not important who gets the credit for these things,' she said.

'Don't be silly,' I said. 'Bess said as much about *The Threepenny Opera*. Afterwards she felt cheated.'

'There isn't going to be that kind of afterwards,' she said. 'Even Brecht has problems getting things on at the moment.'

The baby began to cry and I stood up again to jiggle her, while Grete watched with a kind of envy.

'You are much tougher than I am,' she said.

I knew she was speaking only of my physical health, and shrugged the compliment away. It was something else I wanted her to recognize. I wanted her to confirm I was another creature from herself, a freer spirit and less likely to be a victim. 'Tell me about yourself,' I insisted. 'You never talk about yourself.'

What I wanted was the luxury of talking about Brecht.

When I arrived back in our own flat with the baby, the lights were off, but I found Seryozha sitting huddled in an armchair. 'Why are you sitting in the dark?' I asked him. 'You frightened me.'

'Where have you been to till this hour?' he countered.

I explained rather impatiently. 'You should have knocked on Grete's door. You could see the baby was not in her cot. Where *else* could I have been?'

'You might have been rehearsing,' he said with a glint in his eyes.

'At this hour?'

'Who knows what you may get up to?'

After this we quarrelled, imprecisely, about no issue in particular, and the more unhappily since our words were charged with our knowledge that we had nothing else to give one another.

It must have been the very next morning that Seryozha was arrested.

I don't know what time it was, only that it was still dark outside the windows when the knock came, and that Seryozha seemed to know at once what the uniformed men were doing, while I stood around, stupidly. There were several men, including one of the janitors; I know now that there had to be someone from the flat present to act as a witness. Then, I was surprised to see any familiar face in such an alarming role. The officers themselves were very quiet and friendly. There was a short, lean silent man and another rather older with puffy cheeks.

While I watched, the silent man frisked Seryozha for weapons. Seryozha was in his pyjamas. He held up his hands as instructed, and looked like a frightened boy of twelve. My heart turned over to look at him.

'Get dressed,' said the older man.

'I'll pack,' said Seryozha.

The silent man offered the baby, who had been woken by the bustle of men looking into the bedroom, a piece of hard candy.

I refused curtly. 'She might choke,' I said.

'Take it, take it,' he repeated, either misunderstanding my hesitation or out of some guilt of his own.

Seryozha looked even more frail in his greatcoat and I remembered our quarrel the night before painfully. 'I'm sorry,' I tried to say to him, but he took no account of my words. Tears came to my eyes. I wanted to exchange forgiveness with him, and followed him mutely round the room as he looked for what he needed.

'What are you taking so much stuff for?' called the older man. 'Do you think we shall keep you so long?'

'Where are you taking him?' I cried out, the terror of what was happening suddenly clear to me.

Seryozha now gave me a wan smile.

'You will be told,' said the man with the puffy face.

And then it was over.

I couldn't think what to do, and since there was a line of light under Steffin's door, I knocked there, leaving the baby asleep.

'What will you do?' she asked. 'Who do you know?'

'No one,' I said bleakly.

'Wait till you know where he is,' she advised me.

'I love Seryozha like a child,' I said. 'I can't bear to think of them hurting him. Will they?'

Steffin looked at me oddly, and threw her arms around me. I burst into tears.

5

It was three days before I was summoned to see Seryozha in the local prison, where charges had not yet been preferred. In the interim I learnt something about the country in which I was perching. Apart from Steffin, the doors of my neighbours closed against me as if I had contracted plague. Itzik, whose experience was sharper and nastier than his customary optimism suggested, advised me to say as little as possible. 'My husband has done nothing,' I insisted.

'You know what the saying is? Give us the man and we can make the case,' he told me.

It was the first time I had heard those chilling words, and I was brusque with him. I don't think I understood what he meant until I entered the Moscow prison and saw the red shiny face of the officer behind the desk, and the emaciated hollow-cheeked Seryozha who sat waiting for me between two guards.

'Now we shall clear everything up,' said the officer, smiling with an affability that was not intended to deceive.

Seryozha looked as if he could hardly believe he was seeing me.

'You look terrible,' I said.

'Comrade Bloom,' interrupted the red-faced man, 'we have some questions for you about your husband's Berlin associates.'

'I knew none of them,' I said, too rapidly to carry conviction.

'None of them? Well then, perhaps you can help us identify his French friends,' said the man behind the desk, and I regretted that my wish to conceal had been so obvious.

'It's all right,' said Seryozha with an effort. 'They know about the Skrebenskys.' He sounded unutterably weary. 'They know about everyone I have ever met.'

'It's a farce,' I said angrily.

At this the man behind the desk said, 'I think you would like ten minutes or so to speak intimately together?' and stood up.

I looked at Seryozha uncertainly. Were they really imagining we would spring into scurrilous and incriminating conversation once we were alone?

'The guards will stay,' said the officer before leaving the room.

'What is it like in jail?' I asked then in German.

'In jail?' Seryozha repeated my words, and glanced at the door where the officer had gone. Then he smiled. 'Little Frieda,' he said. It was the first time he had ever seemed older than I was. I don't know what vision of plank-beds, shackles and sleeplessness he had in his thoughts. 'In jail,' he said, 'there is salty food and nothing to drink.'

We held one another's hands tightly and I stared into his eyes which seemed huger than ever, but I can't remember what else we found to say to one another.

A week later he was sent to Irkutsk.

6

It was with Seryozha's three-year sentence in my heart that I read the interview Brecht gave to the press when he arrived in Moscow. Journalists asked him what he thought of the changes in the Soviet Union and he replied that they were enormous, won with great difficulties and all the more important for that. How much does he know, I wondered, about those changes? His face stared out of the paper at me with its scrubby short hair and familiar grin. The eyes behind the tinny spectacles were unreadable. I wondered: Did he know what was happening? And then blankly I was certain that he must know everything.

When Brecht came to Moscow he was met by a delegation of important officials of the Writers' Union and was escorted in their great black cars to the Sovietskaya Hotel. I knew as much from Steffin, who was with him for the first few days. Her excitement was palpable. My own unhappiness at Seryozha's fate could not reach her.

'There is such a programme of festivities,' she explained. 'We have no time to talk. Yesterday we were fêted; next week we are at the opening of the Metro. I wish I felt healthier.'

I saw she was still feverish.

In the event she spent only one night with Brecht at his hotel, before collapsing with blood pouring from her lips, and being taken to a sanatorium. I was sorry to hear of her illness. When she was taken south again to the Crimea, I knew I was more alone than I had ever been in my life. And the post brought no word from Seryozha.

The day of Brecht's reception found me getting into the beaded dress from my Berlin days without any difficulty. My weight had dropped a stone since Seryozha had been taken away. Itzik, who collected me from my apartment, and arranged a friend to look after the child for me, said I looked beautiful, but all I could feel was the emptiness inside me.

'I can't sing,' I said. 'I haven't the heart for it.'

'You'll sing,' he said. 'Whatever else is wrong with you.'

We were invited to one of those blocks of flats built with the declared aim of rewarding enthusiastic workers. The lift was as grand as anything in the decadent West, decorated with rococo curling gilt round the mirrors, the corridors floored in pink and grey marble.

The host was a podgy-fingered man who looked as if he had not done a day's work in his life. I missed his name in marvelling at the height of the ceilings, and the spectacular grandeur of the Empire furniture. I had no idea that such goods continued to exist in Moscow. It was a bit like being let out of prison, or being taken from a black and white film into Hollywood colour. It was a little like my first entry into Westerborg's cabaret. For all my unhappiness, an illicit excitement began to surge round my body.

'There he is,' said Itzik at my side, in his usual ironic tones. 'The greatest anti-Fascist writer we have.'

So it was I saw Bertolt Brecht again. I would have known him anywhere. From his gestures. From his shadow. Just to see the movement of the cigar in his hand as he talked. He was stouter at the neck, perhaps, and his mouth no longer had so sensitive an underlip. He was older, coarser, and by no means ill at ease. None of that, I was horrified to find, mattered in the least. Every line of his body was still dear to me. I would sing well enough, I thought. He will recognize me then.

Meanwhile, there was champagne to drink, and not Soviet champagne, I perceived, but French. There was caviare and salmon eggs. I had been let into a surprising world of privilege for a night. In every world, those inside the holy inner circle live well, and everyone else is destroyed one way or another. What was so strange to me was that Brecht purported to speak for those others outside who were destroyed, while in every society he found himself among those who lived well. And this remained so even in the society where the opportunist struggle for individual good was to have been replaced by some other.

'Eat,' said Itzik, at my side. 'While you can.'

'I don't like to eat before I sing,' I said.

130

I was nervous because I recognized so many faces around me from Berlin days, and heard German on every side. So I ate very little, and prepared for the moment when I would be summoned to the piano.

When I sang in German the audience quietened a little, and I watched Brecht turn his head in recognition. I looked straight into his eyes, and sang 'Surabaya Johnnie' in memory of Bess, and the 'Pirate' song in memory of Lenya. Then I sang a new song of my own for which Itzik had written the music, a song about women who don't live well when they only think about love. It was a Marxist song in its way, but that wasn't why the audience listened.

Afterwards people bustled up to me, even though the next piece of entertainment was that of a distinguished classical pianist, and the organisers' faces were urging everyone to take seats. Brecht was among them. 'Frieda,' he said in a muffled voice. 'When can we meet?'

'I am free,' I said.

It was not what I had intended to say.

'We must eat together tomorrow,' he said. His black eyes went cunningly over my face for signs of what had been happening to me. I tried to look cool and friendly, but there was not a piece of my body that was indifferent to the tone of his voice.

'How long will you be here?' I asked.

'About two months.'

I did my best to conceal the flood of happiness that went through me at the news.

'I had flu for the first weeks,' he said. 'There's a lot to arrange.'

'I heard you were in New York.'

'A disaster,' he told me. 'They only want the most vulgar naturalism. I'm sick and tired of all that foolishness.'

'You had no trouble getting a US visa?'

'Weigel's Jewish descent was for once a help,' he said with a grin.

I asked formally about Weigel's health, but he was impatiently curious about me. 'What are you up to?'

'I don't get much work here,' I confessed. The homesickness

131

was sharp and painful in my voice. He heard it and shook his head disapprovingly.

'What about Carola Neher?' he asked me.

I frowned.

'How does she manage?' he continued. 'I hear she is rather stout now. They don't think highly of her here.'

I had worse news of Carola Neher but I did not speak of it then. 'Tell me what you've seen in the theatre?' I asked him, to divert his attention.

'The Chinese actor Mei Lanfang with his troupe. He plays girls' parts splendidly.'

There were other people around us now.

'Let's meet,' he said.

'It's spring. We can go for a walk on the Lenin Hills,' I suggested.

He hesitated.

'Let me send a car for you,' he urged.

7

Would he have been so eager to renew our acquaintance if Steffin had been in Moscow? I think he might. My survival without him had given an edge to his interest. He was always most attentive towards women who thought of leaving him. For my part, I slept not one minute of the night that separated our meeting from the one we had arranged for the following day. I simply lay on my bed and looked up at the ceiling.

He was in the black car that came for me, dressed in unfamiliar furs, and the cumbersome clothes separated us as we took our places on the back seat side by side. Behind us, at a distance that was hardly discreet, another car followed. There were not so many cars in Moscow in those days.

It was April; the sunshine glinted off the wet trees and for a while we drove through the dazzling streets in silence, and stared out at the beauty of central Moscow with its yellow painted houses and golden cupolas as if for the first time.

'I've been trying to get a film part here for Helli,' he said. 'She would like to be here.'

'I gather you didn't like New York,' I said.

'The Left-wing theatres in the West,' he shrugged. 'They're run by hacks. They have the manners of Broadway producers without their experience.'

Then a strange silence fell between us, as Brecht stared moodily out of the window, and I wondered what I could safely report to him of the confused feelings that racked me.

We left the car at the foot of the Lenin Hills and climbed up to get a look at Moscow, still dazzling in the afternoon sunshine. The cold air bit at my throat, for all the splendour of the day, as the heat went out of the sun. Brecht puffed a little.

'Too many cigars,' I told him and he smiled at me approvingly.

'You look very healthy.'

'Something has to go well,' I said.

We continued to walk upwards, and I pointed out the River Moskva, a grey snake catching the last light. Then we stood and looked downwards.

'I'm really surprised how civilized things are here, how many things are available,' he said.

'Not for a German singer,' I said sharply. 'We live poorly here.' I wanted to describe the situation accurately. I wasn't thinking of asking him for help, but I wanted him to know how things really were. He misunderstood.

'There's talk of a German theatre here,' he said.

'Only feeble talk. It won't happen,' I said, angry at some constraint that kept me from pouring out what I wanted to say. He seemed to feel it was his position to instruct me.

'You are lucky to be out of Germany,' he said sharply. 'They are rounding up Jews and Communists and sending them to the East. There are worse rumours.'

'I know what is happening in Germany,' I said.

'No, you don't,' he said. 'A friend of mine went back, so he didn't know. Some trouble he had with the authorities here. They didn't like what he was teaching. Can you imagine the folly? He could have gone anywhere, and he went back to Germany. He was a Jew. Of course he is now in a camp.'

'I know what is happening to Jews,' I said.

'Have you had news of your father?' he asked me quietly.

I had not thought of him for a long while, and I said as much.

'I think you will find he is no longer at his old address,' he said.

I didn't know what to say.

'Be sensible,' he continued. 'Here people are working hard. Most people. It's a big country, neglected for centuries. Stalin is doing what he can. And he is the only bulwark we have against the Nazis.' He sounded tired, as if he had said as much many times. 'The tide is rising all over Europe,' he said. Then he put an arm round my shoulders, and turned me towards him. 'I'd like to make you happy,' he said.

The temperature had dropped since we left the car, and the grass had begun to crunch under my feet. The light had gone out of the air long since, except for the sky in the west. In the falling darkness, the air was bitterly cold and cut my throat as I kept swallowing again and again. 'We must get back,' I said.

The thought that he might still care what happened to me made me intensely aware of how long it had been since anyone touched me with love. He saw as much and smiled at me confidently. Then I astonished him.

'They have taken my husband to jail,' I said. For a moment I saw his small black eyes shift craftily behind his glasses. 'What can he possibly have done?' he asked then, carefully.

A laugh tore at my throat. 'What makes you think he has done anything?'

'If he has been convicted, I'm sure it wasn't without ample evidence,' he said.

We were walking down the hill now, his arm still round my shoulders, comfortingly. But I wrenched myself away. 'It isn't true,' I said.

'Frieda, poor girl, I know what you mean,' he said, pulling me back towards him. 'But there must have been something all the same. I know it might not be a crime but they have to be so careful here.'

'To safeguard the Revolution, you mean,' I said, unable to keep the bitterness out of my voice. 'They have to root out traitors.'

'I don't say he is any such thing. Their caution often seems disproportionate,' he tried to agree with me.

'There was nothing suspicious about him,' I said. 'He just wanted to get on with his work.'

'To be taken to jail –' He hesitated. 'He must have represented some kind of threat. To the Party.'

'No,' I said again.

His arm fell away from my shoulders. We could see the lights of the parked car now, as we walked down the hill together. 'Frieda,' he said reproachfully, as if my words were no more than childish obstinacy.

I said nothing.

'I'm not angry,' he said after a while.

I made a noise something like a laugh.

'A little impatient perhaps,' he said. 'I read so much more on these matters.'

135

'Don't you know,' I replied bitterly, 'anyone can be made to say anything? Why do they follow *you*, by the way?' I asked him as we went on walking side by side.

He did not ask me whom I meant by 'they'. There were two cars parked below us, and the second had been following us from my flat.

'I am followed everywhere,' he said. 'It's amusing. In Denmark I am followed because they think I am making anti-Nazi propaganda. In America they think I'm a Communist. Who knows what they think here?' He stopped and turned me towards him as if he would have liked to shake me. 'It's a big country, Frieda. You don't understand how difficult it is for Stalin to keep it from flying apart. Some bad things may have to be justified.'

'Fascism could say the same.'

'The cruelties of fascism cannot be justified,' he said. His eyes glinted blackly. 'Stalin is the only one who can stop Hitler, and that is the most important thing now. His boots are taking over Europe.'

I said no more. I was not persuaded by his arguments, but the trouble was I still loved him, and everything else had become irrelevant as we spoke. I couldn't help it. The shoulders, the turn of his head, everything was dear to me.

'About Grete Steffin,' I said, a little disingenuously. 'She has been a very good friend to me.'

'I'm sorry she's ill,' he said impatiently. 'I need her.'

'She has been a good friend to me,' I repeated as if to ease my conscience.

'Come and stay a night with me. For old times,' he said, as I had known he would.

I should like to be able to say that I refused. I couldn't. In my loneliness he was all there was that felt like home. He was all the good life I still hoped to have. He was affection, warmth and love. I had invested his body alone with those qualities.

'All right,' I said.

8

For days after that encounter with Brecht I was aware of the world about me with a peculiar intensity. Spring in Moscow is always heady. Now, even walking through the dingy local park past the beer kiosks, I was filled with the beauty of the new green leaves, and the aureole of sunlight caught in the black twigs. The mildness of the air, even when damp, was intoxicating; the brightness everywhere blinding; the puddles like pools of silver.

I took my daughter into the centre of Moscow to show her the great river moving again, and the whole city seemed to be made of water and sky. When the child smiled at me, her small milky teeth made her face as enchanting as an elf. I sat and brushed her long, pale hair until it shone. It was as if a wintry metallic lid over me had been removed so that I could feel again.

Almost as if to absolve me from the pleasure I was taking, a letter came that week from Seryozha. From Irkutsk. His exile was less arduous than I had feared. He described rows of carts pulled by ponies; markets where stalls gleamed with fresh fish; stalls of watermelons and strings of onions, heaped piles of cucumber, parsley, and radishes. Even a convict, he wrote, could take pleasure in the wild flowers that grew on the outskirts of the town. It was very surprising and the relief of hearing so much made me even happier.

About this relief, Itzik was sceptical, and we came close to quarrelling about it. 'I hope you're right,' he said.

He pulled his trilby down over his forehead and played gloomy folk melodies. He had no reason to be rehearsing with me any more; it was pure kindness, a wish to keep me in practice and hopeful, and after an angry outburst at his failure to respond to my good news, I looked closely into his face, as if for the first time. I had always thought of him as ugly, because he wore thick glasses, and behaved towards me without the least flirtatiousness.

Now I saw his cheeks were wryly lined and his lips had a humorous curve, and I recognized his concern.

'Are you married?' I asked, on an impulse.

'No longer,' he said. 'I lost my wife in Kiev.'

'To another man?'

'A man with a knife.'

He stopped playing the piano.

'How long ago?' I asked, frightened.

'More than ten years,' he said.

'In the civil war?'

'Afterwards,' he said. 'Nothing political. Ukrainians don't like Jews.'

'Don't be such a nationalist,' I said.

Brecht had been particularly scathing about the nationalism of Jews of his acquaintance who were only interested in the Nazis' enmity to their race, and had begun to put their faith in a state of their own in Palestine.

Itzik shrugged. 'Jews have problems here. There's a history. You don't have to be a Zionist to know it. What about in Germany?'

'That,' I said rather primly, 'is an expression of the class conflict.'

'Tell that to Jews who aren't bankers. Most aren't,' he said, and played another mocking little tune as he swung round to smile at me. 'Here. You know the joke. You don't go to synagogue, you eat pork, how do you know you're Jewish?' he said.

I looked blank.

'It's in my passport,' he explained with a melancholy smile.

'But things are different here now. So many Bolsheviks were Jews,' I insisted, disposed to argue in my new outgoing frame of mind.

He struck a jangling chord. 'Maybe even that will be held against them one day,' he said.

Brecht was busy meeting important figures in the Moscow film world, and I wasn't surprised that he had little time to see me. After a few days, I telephoned him at the Sovietskaya Hotel. He arranged to see me, much to my surprise, that very evening. 'Before I go,' he said.

'Why? Going so soon? What has changed your plans?' I asked him.

'I'll send a car. We'll talk later,' he said.

When I put down the telephone, a pain I had almost forgotten suffused my whole body.

Don't ruin tonight, I told myself as severely as I could, as I put out my simplest clothes, knowing he always preferred them. Enjoy what there is. What else does anyone have? But as soon as he brought me into his room, and I saw all the untidy evidence of his departure, a wave of tears rose up in me. He was going. He was taking his love away from me. And I burst out with questions I had determined not to ask.

He was drinking brandy and smoking a cigar, and his eyes behind his glasses were round and innocent.

'Have you seen everyone you wanted to see?' I asked.

'I went to see Knorrin,' he told me.

A prickle of alarm went through me at that, since Knorrin was known to be close to the leadership. At the same time I remembered we were in a hotel that was certain to be under KGB surveillance.

'I thought you wanted to do a great many things here,' I said, controlling myself and smiling as winningly as I could.

'I can do more in the West,' he said. 'They are going to finance a magazine for me.'

I sat on the bed, suddenly tired.

He came over to me and put a hand on me. 'Don't let's waste our time together,' he said.

I let him put a hand between my legs, I let my body respond as it would. Yet inside another voice nagged and wondered, even as we made love. What is it he promised to do in return?

I saw him once more quite by chance on Ulitsa Gorkova a couple of days later. Evidently his departure had been delayed. I had been visiting someone about a job in the theatre. The official had been perfectly friendly. If I felt a little off-colour, he could arrange a trip to a union dacha in the south where I might like to recuperate from whatever distressed me. He would help willingly. But there was nothing for me in the Moscow theatre. We were in the open air and I told Brecht as much in a burst of resentment.

'Come back with me to Denmark,' he suggested. 'I could arrange that.'

'Maybe,' I said.

'Steffin has decided to return,' he encouraged me.

'What does Weigel say?' I asked.

'She understands,' he said.

'Does she?' I asked.

And then, in my disappointment, I added, 'America would be another matter. If it were possible.'

This angered him. 'Don't you learn anything?' he said. 'You aren't self-sufficient. You can't make your own way. Be sensible. As a group we can survive together.' He bent, and kissed me on the forehead. 'Groups survive. Remember that.'

9

I remember coming in the day after that meeting with Brecht to find the postman had brought me news from somewhere far east of Irkutsk. It was a formal note from a camp commander, and at first I could not make it out. Then I understood there had been an accident. A terrible accident. Seryozha was dead.

I had no one to tell except Itzik, and I crossed town to find him with my child in my arms. He seemed to know what I was going to say before I spoke, and took the child from me. She snuggled into his arms and he took her away into the kitchen to give her milk and a biscuit. I tried to compose myself.

When he came back, he said a neighbour would look after her for me and I nodded dumbly. He patted my knee, and took off his glasses. Once again I saw how attractively handsome was his mouth. His eyes, now they were naked, were brown and large as my own. I let him kiss me without guilt, without desire, without expectation of pleasure, simply to shut out the blackness which threatened to drown me. There is something about the discovery of death which only sexual love can heal.

Afterwards, I wondered to myself: perhaps it is that blackness which men of great imagination have all the time in their heart, and that is why they have to seek pleasure so desperately with any woman who can arouse their lust.

And Itzik said, 'I understand. Don't say anything.'

So it was we came to live together, that funny, rash little man, whose talents I only half appreciated, whose kindness and warmth saved my life in the next few years.

From time to time I wrote to Brecht. Steffin, I heard, was back in Denmark. I only had one note from him. His speeches to the anti-Fascist congresses in Paris were widely reported, and seemed admirable. When the Spanish war started, I heard of him in Spain from a friend of Itzik who returned with bleak stories of internecine rivalries and betrayals. I don't think Brecht went to the Front himself.

I continued to write letters to Brecht, and sent him the songs I still wrote in German. You must try to understand: I had no chance to sing them, and I needed to imagine someone receiving them in order to go on writing. To go on living, on the other hand, I needed Itzik's daily wisdom.

Perhaps wisdom is not exactly the word for Itzik's reckless propensity to say what he thought, and make the jokes that amused him. And yet he had a generosity of spirit that made the years we were together among the sweetest of my life, for all the frustrations.

The surprise was that Itzik survived untroubled as long as he did.

Sometimes we planned to leave the country, thinking of America where, for all its evils, Itzik's music might be valued, and they would love my sharp little verses. It was all a daydream, and my child spoke Russian now rather than German, and if I still studied to perfect my English I no longer thought it was likely I would stand on a stage and sing again. My hair had begun to go grey. I was not yet forty, but I felt an old woman. I have never since felt as old as I did then in my thirties, living with a dear friend. Even now I don't feel as old as I did then.

One day, some of Itzik's friends invited us to take a meal with them at the Metropole. I had heard about the Metropole and the people who frequented the restaurant.

'I don't really want to go,' I said. 'It's a place for black marketeers and their women. And KGB men,' I added, as an afterthought.

'It's the closest we get to a Berlin night life,' he observed. 'Anyway, there's a woman I want to meet. She is very interested in Yiddish theatre, and she knows you.'

'She won't know me now,' I said, laughing. And it was that vanity that made me reluctant to go. There was no longer any flash and glory in me. I didn't want to go where people took pleasure in showing off their bodies and exchanging gaiety.

He laid a finger to his nose, in imitation of thieves, knowingly. 'The American woman has arranged everything. She is even sending a car,' he said.

142

It was winter, and the offer of a car was irresistible.

How, I wondered, should I *dress* to go to the Metropole? I didn't want to compete with the young and glamorous. I searched through my wardrobe and chose a slightly worn silk. It hung tightly over my hips. I will try no more than that, I thought. It is always great efforts that are disappointed.

There was a line outside the restaurant as we drew up outside but it parted for us. A doorman in braided uniform stepped through, made a way for us, and in response to him a door opened. Soon a waiter found a table, on which I saw, with bemused wonder, beautifully starched tablecloths and napkins, and a glitter of silver and crystal.

It was not as busy as I had expected. Most people would arrive in half an hour when the theatres finished. There were plenty of Moscow girls in the restaurant, all looking pretty enough but provincial, in spite of their feathers and beads. I, on the other hand, looked and felt an ill-dressed woman of thirty-five. There were no eyes for me. The jaunty music as it changed from foxtrot to rumba made me miserable, as it reminded me of a life that was over.

Itzik ordered vodka for both of us.

'Why so gloomy?' he asked.

I shook my head. 'I'm happy enough as we are,' I said. 'All this upsets me.'

He shook his head at my mood. And then a woman of about fifty, dressed in a spangly dress that clung like molten gold to her stout figure and yet remained curiously elegant, came over to our table.

'Well, Frieda Bloom, for heaven's sake,' she said, and I recognized the American producer who had met me in that Moscow theatre years before. Itzik stood up for her, and I realized she was the woman he had arranged to meet.

The lights dimmed, spotlights illuminated the fountain, the band began to play. Not all the dancers could handle the alien steps, and I watched them with impatience. Itzik was not a great dancer, and when he offered to take me on to the floor, I refused curtly. I had no desire to show off my skills. For one thing, I

143

wasn't dressed for display, and the dance floor invited display. I was tormented by a sense of what I had once been, and would never be again.

While these emotions ran through my blood a young woman came on to the centre of the floor, and began to sing. The producer bent across to me, and said in her awkward German, 'It would be marvellous if you would sing something for us.'

'I'm horribly out of practice,' I said, flushing. 'And I'm not dressed for it.'

'Go on,' encouraged Itzik. 'I'll play for you. Why not?'

At this I stood up in a kind of desperation to escape, and one of my heels caught in the hem of my dress, which tore up one seam. I had been going to refuse; now I had an excuse to leave the table without offending Itzik and I almost ran away to look for the powder room.

If I had been less distressed I would have been intrigued by the tawdry western splendours of that room where young women touched up their lipstick and stood gossiping as they admired their reflections. As I watched, an attendant with a needle and thread was repairing the torn hem of another shiny dress and would gladly have helped with mine, but instead I collapsed on a pink-seated chair and began to cry absurdly, as if I were once again a young girl myself.

'What is it, my dear?' asked the attendant, in a soft Georgian voice that only made me weep the more.

How could I explain? I was crying for the life I had not had, that had been taken from me. For everything I could do once and would never do again. I brought my tears under control, blew my nose and spoke without any expectation of being understood. 'It will never be my turn now,' I said.

The Georgian looked at me and blinked, and I saw that she was beautiful in the style of her region with hair heavily tinted with henna, but a broad face that reminded me in some odd way of my almost forgotten Aunt Clara. 'What's the matter with you? Don't be so silly!' she reproached me.

I blinked and approached the mirror. 'Go on,' she urged. In my ears a voice from another life urged me with her: 'Loosen your hair, undo a button or two, paint your lips.'

144

And at my feet, as I repaired my face, she deftly repaired my dress, and as she mended a hem and clucked over my tears, it was as if my almost forgotten aunt were once again my mentor. After all, why shouldn't I sing?

So I sang at the Metropole, an old German ballad of my own, whose words I thought I hardly remembered, but which flowed back freely as soon as Itzik began to play. And the audience listened as they always had.

'You still have the voice,' said the American woman as I returned to the table, stunned by the applause. 'And we can easily fix the hair.'

It seemed she was willing to act as our sponsor in America, always supposing it was possible to get an exit visa from Russia.

Itzik squeezed my hand under the table, and I smiled back at him, responding to the dream in his eyes more than the probabilities. For Itzik, America was the golden land, as it had been for his cousins who escaped there under the Tsars; for me it was the land of the Alabama song, and Chicago, a place of stockyards and bootleggers. Still, I would have gone anywhere with him. The American woman seemed kindly, and I was to be grateful for her offer of sponsorship.

Yet, for all my unworldliness, I was not overpowered with optimism. I knew very little about the quota restrictions on US immigration which she began to explain to me, but I knew one thing of which she seemed ignorant: it was impossible to imagine under what conditions Itzik would be given an exit visa to leave the Soviet Union.

It was 1937, the year they call in Russia the Year of Yezhov. In that year, the purges tightened. Men who had been released from prison, or allowed back from exile, were taken back into custody. Millions more who never expected to find themselves in any kind of trouble were that year trawled into the same net. And among those who had relied for so many years on a charmed life was my poor Itzik, who never lived to see the America he had always dreamed about.

They came for him as they had for Seryozha, and though he tried to smile and make a joke as they took him through the door, I clung to him so strenuously that my hands had to be forcibly opened by the guards. Afterwards, I sat where they had roughly pushed me until it was morning. The blood in my wrists felt cold. When my daughter came out sleepily to look for breakfast, there were deep red nail marks where my hands had balled into fists.

I was never allowed to see Itzik in prison. The packages I queued up to deliver to him were accepted with a blank face. There were rumours he had been sent to Kolyma, but I think now that he never survived the first weeks in the Lubianka.

When the Nazis flooded out over Europe, pushing into Denmark and Poland, Stalin made a pact with Hitler.

Later it was said the pact was a clever Georgian trick, only intended to give Stalin time to develop his army, but in 1939 all we refugees from Germany saw was the Russian army going into Poland and the three Baltic Republics, and shaking hands with our enemies. When Stalin launched into war with Finland our confusion deepened. Even after all we knew, and in my case even after the loss of two husbands, we had still believed in Stalin at least as an ally against Hitler. We were stunned by such an enormous defection. Not that we spoke of such things. We were by now afraid even to spend time together since we knew how readily we were suspected; the more since opponents of Hitler were no longer counted automatically as friends.

All this I understood at a remove, in stunned misery, as the months went by and my daughter grew in front of me. I taught her to read the English script as well as the Cyrillic she learnt in school. I might have confused her, but luckily she was very bright.

I cannot remember when I had my first letter from Brecht, but it came from Sweden shortly after the invasion of Poland. He had been living in the house of a sculptress in Stockholm, where his active work against the Nazis was evidently seen as endangering Swedish neutrality.

It was an extraordinary letter, full of energy and certainty. He was writing *Mother Courage*, I remember; he described the plot to me, and mentioned other things he was busy with. It was an extraordinary act of faith to go on writing plays at such a moment when there were no theatres to put them on, and little enough hope of getting out of Europe.

I suppose he already saw that his only way out was going to lie through the USSR, and that was why he wrote to me; others in Moscow received letters. He had not yet applied formally for a quota visa to the States, he told me, although he had been thinking of it; he found the questions he was required to answer degrading, and in any case he could not leave Europe without Steffin, who was now so seriously tubercular that there was no hope of getting an American visa for her. He repeated several times that he could not leave without her. Then he asked me in a cursory way to arrange some minor publishing business for him. I did what I could, moved by his loyalty to my poignant, quirky friend. I think there may have also been a mention of another actress, the beautiful Ruth Berlau. No doubt he was in love with her then and she with him. There was always someone for whom he felt a profound romantic attachment. But these essentials of his spiritual metabolism were less important to me than his safety. I wrote back several letters urging him to leave for the States and reminding him of his duty to survive.

For my own part, I worked now in the canteen of the Union of Theatrical Workers, and my main concern was to dress my child and get through the long months of winter. The loss of Itzik lay like a stone in my chest.

10

In melting snows, in a Russia not yet at war but confused, apprehensive and unhappy, I was astonished one day to run into Brecht on the streets of Moscow. It was April 1941, somewhere near the river, somewhere near Lavrushinsky. He was standing talking to someone with great urgency, arguing, gesturing with a blunt short cigar. I recognized the man. He was a friend of Grete Steffin. I had known his wife quite well; she had recently been sent to Kazakhstan. When we were introduced a few weeks earlier, I had shared a nervous joke with him about our status as survivors of our dearest loves. Now I stood for a while and watched Brecht talking to him before crossing to make myself known. Brecht's face was unusually drawn beneath his Moscow fur hat. He nodded rather than smiled at me. His eyes did not flicker over my face. They found my own in an odd, still stare. He looked almost drugged with fatigue.

'Grete is ill,' he said at once. 'Too ill to go any further.' He seemed at his wits' end. 'We have boat tickets from Vladivostok,' he said. 'She is too ill to take the journey. I don't know what to do.' His face was bleak, without even the grimmest suggestion of a grin.

'Where are Weigel and Berlau?' asked his friend.

'With the children. In the hotel. I am going back to the hospital,' he said.

A flood of conjecture rushed over me. 'Let me walk along with you,' I said, taking his arm.

He hardly seemed to see me.

As we went along the streets of slush, he wanted only to speak of Steffin. He spoke of her courage. His refusal to leave her. She was his little soldier of the Revolution. I pressed his arm, and listened to his monotone of anxiety as we walked. Then he spoke of his responsibility to Weigel and the children. 'We must leave in the next forty-eight hours. It is our only chance to get the boat,' he said. 'And I still have to organize exit visas.'

'That won't be easy,' I said.

At this his eyes focused on me for the first time. We had come to the hospital, and were standing close by the entrance, where at that moment an ambulance was delivering a woman who looked close to death. We watched the stretcher going into the hospital doors.

'What are you doing these days?' he asked me. 'Thank you for your letters, by the way. I haven't always replied.'

I shrugged wearily.

For a moment he took in my own separate desperation. I had written to him about Itzik, and perhaps he remembered as much. It was cold by then; all the afternoon sunlight had gone, and I think it was beginning to rain. He looked at me with some kindness as if at this juncture he could acknowledge me as a fellow mortal confronted by death. I cannot know what he intended then, but he suggested I go to the hotel, where Weigel and Berlau would be glad to see me. I would have liked to see Steffin, but I knew it was impossible.

That evening I turned up at the hotel as I had promised, and found a scene of dismay and tension. The luggage with which they intended to go onward was only there in part; the rest was still in Moscow railway station. When I entered they were expecting someone from the hotel staff who was supposed to sort out the problem. I introduced myself, and for a moment saw Weigel suspect me, even though I spoke good German; then she remembered me from Berlin, passed a hand uncertainly over her own hair, and made me welcome.

She had the same tough face; it was by now a disturbing toughness, almost stupid in its determination; her stamina was not yet impaired. Later on, when I saw *Mother Courage* I marvelled at how in her own person she prefigured that character as she dealt with contingencies. She administered the whole caravan of Brecht's family like Courage's cart.

She made me welcome. We drank the poor coffee sent up by the hotel; we waited. Weigel said little. After a time I became aware of

Ruth Berlau, who had come in with the children from another room. She was drinking from a flask of brandy. I disliked her instantly. Her beauty was of the open and healthy sort which bespoke an alien temperament; in turn, she had no time for me, once my identity was established. In times of stress and suspense there is little to say about anything but the anxious matter itself. I observed that in their anxiety Weigel and Berlau were not enemies; that in some way they had made joint cause. They spoke little of Grete.

Brecht did not return until it was too late to catch the Metro. I prayed that my child would sleep without anxiety, and waited. When at last he arrived, we could see from his face that the news was bad.

'She is too ill,' he said simply. 'I have left her tickets and money, and a friend will see her on to the train if it is possible. Meanwhile I will go and see about exit visas in the morning.'

Then he looked at me. 'Let me see what I can do for you at the same time.'

So it was, miraculously, that I came to be on that train going towards Vladivostok.

I took nothing with me except my notebooks, and clothes for the child. She was a little querulous, and I was impatient. We were fortunate to be leaving and I knew as much.

I remember the first night on that train vividly. The train stank of disinfectant, and we crawled through desolate countryside; I stood at the window looking out at miles of mud; even the birch trees looked thin, and the stations we went through were deserted beyond the rickety wooden footplanks. We were heading into central Russia. The skies were grey and overcast. In the suspense of wondering whether guards would come on board and take off my child and me at the last minute, there was no room for any other uncertainty.

I suppose a question may have come into my heart: How was it Brecht was able to do what no one else could? What had he offered, what could he offer, that made it possible for us all to get on a train and escape a country that was as hard to leave as Nazi Germany?

In the end of that long night I stopped wondering about anything. I was merely travelling, onwards and for several days. The train rocked from side to side, shook, speeded up, slowed again, and as night fell lights flashed at the windows. The child mercifully slept.

It was a question of survival. I should not survive the next trawl for suspects. I had not the spirit to survive the camps. And for survival, as Brecht had always taught, much is permitted and may always be required.

We faced a long journey. Vladivostok was the only port from which boats still sailed to the United States. I was not at first with the main Brecht party, who all travelled first class; but after a time I was allowed to join them. Their section was part of an old and luxurious train, and there were small salons where people played chess and listened to the radio. It was cold, however. Weigel and Berlau were wearing fur coats which Brecht had bought for them with the roubles he had to spend in Russia. There were separate sleeping compartments for Berlau, and for Weigel and for the children; with a little pressure, I could have had one of my own too, but I preferred to listen to my child sleeping. Her breathing comforted me.

And I needed that animal comfort. Every time the train stopped, I was aware that soldiers could come on board and take us off; there were also messages from poor Grete Steffin, sent by a friend at her bedside, giving all the details of her condition, which Brecht received eagerly. He sent telegrams back to her, through the interpreter who travelled with us.

'What can he say in them?' I wondered.

Weigel told me gloomily, 'He asks her to sleep and eat.'

The messages from Steffin's friend recorded every detail of her day. These included a glass of champagne, and a wish to wash her hair on the day she died.

I remember we were travelling through Siberia, along a stretch of water of great beauty, when the message came. And Brecht stood for a while, looking out at that great Lake Beikal, and saying nothing. Weigel stood at his side as protectively as some great mother beast in the presence of a child in pain.

151

I had nothing to say. The chill of death had already entered me; I remember Itzik saying that Yiddish was a language of ghosts and that he had more friends among the dead than the living. It was becoming my case. I remembered how little Steffin had asked from life. I thought of her broken comb, her unrepairable stockings, and her worn-out shoes. I thought of the cheap ring Brecht had given her as a sign of their early love; and the way she had worn it on her finger, even when her hand swelled. Visions of her pert face pushed into an oxygen mask, and then blue in death, haunted me with hallucinatory sharpness.

I knew then that Brecht was capable of love, and for him love had little to do with the sensual life which no doubt remained strong in him; that for him it was a tender emotion closer to the need to protect than the wish for protection.

He disappeared for two days after the news of Steffin's death. He disappeared, I noticed, into Weigel's compartment. Berlau could be found looking impatient and smoking heavily in the salons where people hung around and gossiped. I could see she was angry that this was so, when Weigel emerged and we shared a samovar of tea.

Naturally we spoke of the European situation. Warnings of the Wehrmacht's impending attack on Russia must have been reaching the Kremlin at the very time we were perching at the Metropolitan Hotel. Berlau told me she had heard as much, even as she went about Moscow trying to collect Brecht's royalties. The rumours were everywhere discounted. She also told me Brecht had gone to visit the powerful Hungarian, George Lucaks, who had often been critical of Brecht's work, and was of no help now. She had tried and failed to get news of Carola Neher. Weigel remained harsh and silent through most of our conversation. Once she said, almost to herself, 'He is getting over it. He will be all right.'

11

My daughter spent the journey on board ship in a fever most of the time; a germ, I suppose, since the food aboard ship was fresh and plentiful. Weigel looked after her for some of the time, which was the more generous since her own conditions were uncomfortable.

We were aboard a small Swedish freighter, and the close members of Brecht's family had been asked to share a cabin, though Berlau quickly made other arrangements with a radio officer, who found her a cabin of her own, no doubt misunderstanding her intentions. Brecht therefore had some privacy, though Weigel and the children suffered.

As the ship steamed south towards Manila, Brecht's children developed mumps. For all that, Brecht remained the centre of attention. His simplest need was a demand that everyone recognized. Every morning began with his wishes, and his moods shaped the course of the day. His sadness demanded cheering: his energy had to be answered with the same force: his spirit needed endless feeding. Berlau and Weigel were so used to turning all their vitality towards him that they seemed unaware of this grotesque insistence. It was rather like being in the presence of a much-loved eighteen-month-old child, whose mother only has time to herself when the child sleeps. Now I had lived a long while alone, and I knew solitude well: I was used to its freedom. Such unquestioning obedience repelled me.

It may seem strange that it was at this point in our lives, when I saw so much more humanity in Brecht than I ever had, that I should reject him for the first time. Yet when he asked for my love on board that ship I could not give him what he asked.

I don't know why he wanted it so insistently, when both Ruth Berlau and Weigel clearly lived every hour of their days for him. Perhaps it was because he sensed my attention was drawn elsewhere, when my child was ill. Perhaps, as he knew he was entering a new land and a language he had not mastered, he felt a need to establish a wider net of power. And perhaps he sensed that power was slipping from him. At any rate, when he came one night to my room, I refused him.

'Frieda,' he reproached me, almost incredulously.

And I knew he needed my declaration of love, like an old man needs the sweetness of youth to sustain him, but I could give him nothing.

PART FIVE

NEW YORK

'For we went, changing countries oftener than shoes . . .'

Brecht: 'To Those Born Later'

1

Certainly, Brecht was a genius. The voice in his poems makes me melt even now; those of us who borrowed it were doing no more than that. As to the rest: even in more commonplace relationships there is always one who loves, and one who is loved . . . At any rate, I made my decision not to become Brecht's victim on board ship.

When we came ashore gratefully in San Pedro, among the gardens and vines of southern California, I had made up my mind to separate myself from the Brecht caravan. I looked at palm trees, citrus fruit and ice-plant; sticky ferns unrolling their fronds; and weird, flowering birds of paradise. I saw the great sun falling like a ball of red gold into the ocean. And I knew I was looking out across a part of the planet altogether more alien to me than the snows of Moscow. Argyle Street, where the Brecht family perched, offered me nothing.

Brecht was unafraid of Hollywood. If Berlau and Weigel were troubled about what were likely to be their own roles in keeping Brecht's enterprise going, they made no sign in those first bewildering weeks. For my part, I had a sponsor in New York, and no intention of remaining part of Brecht's life.

I wanted my freedom. And if loneliness was to be the necessary price of that freedom I was prepared to pay it. I had become used to life alone with a small child, and it held no terrors for me. If Brecht had been less preoccupied with making contacts in the film industry, he might have held me in California even then; but, apart from a bout of irritability in which he taunted me with my lack of staying power and warned me again that I should not survive living alone, he did not bother to argue with me. If he had charged me with ingratitude, I should never have escaped.

There was just a powdering of grey in my hair when I arrived in New York, but it was still thick and bristly; and that oily skin, once so condemned by my nanny, had kept its resilience. Maybe I was a little fatter, as a result of the Soviet diet. But my spirit was alive and hopeful.

The first person I looked up, after my sponsor, was Lotte Lenya. She and Kurt had moved to New York from Paris in good order and good time, and Kurt had fallen on his feet. They had a country house in Hudson Valley, much loved at the time by theatrical folk who wanted a bit of privacy not too far away from Manhattan.

I arrived in clothes bought in New York, a little hesitant as a result of my Moscow years, and Lenya threw her arms around me with enthusiasm.

'You haven't changed,' she said to me.

'Don't be silly,' I said, falling with relief into vulgar street German. 'I'm nearly ten years older.'

'I can't believe that,' she said.

Lenya looked marvellous. There were laughter lines in her cheeks. Her hair was cut straight and full. She wore a black sweater crossing easily over her breasts. She had all her teeth, and they looked whiter than I remembered them, perhaps because she had a Californian tan. The backs of her hands were freckled, and her nails were long and red.

'What is that mark on your wrists?' I asked, without tact. I had seen those slash marks many times in Russia.

She nodded in admission of their meaning. 'Yes. It was when Kurt and I were apart,' she said. 'I hate to be alone. Have you been alone?'

I told her as matter of factly as I could what had happened to me. When I came to the loss of Itzik, I wept. She patted my hand.

In those days the tally of friends destroyed was too daily a horror to register the disappearance of a stranger with more than such mute acknowledgement.

'Every day people disappear like that. Kurt cannot sleep,' she said.

Perhaps it is hard for anyone now to recapture the peculiar toughness we all needed then in that terrifying human moment when Hitler and his triumphant troops were surveying the world about them with such lordly certainty of power.

'At least you are here and the child is safe,' she said.

'Yes,' I replied.

158

There was some uneasiness in my voice, because I had begun to worry about my daughter. Her prettiness had been lessened by losing her front teeth, and the liveliness which had made her so precocious a child as she mastered first one language, then another, was no longer so evident. I understood that she had seen two fathers disappear, and that she must hold me and my world responsible. Even as she stuffed a chocolate cake into her mouth her blue eyes were clear and judgemental.

'We are all safe here,' repeated Lenya, pushing another plate of cakes across towards the child. She had chosen against children herself, and perhaps that accounted for an unfamiliar sadness in her voice.

It cannot have been more than a month or so after that conversation that America too was in the war.

That year I improved my English. English was easier for me than Russian, naturally: I had heard it in my childhood from my nanny. My daughter and I lived modestly by New York standards, but every minute of my life seemed beautiful to me. I know some survivors of those horrors felt guilt later but most of us tasted the brilliance of sunshine in Manhattan with relief, as the news of one defeat after another filled us with the fear that the whole world would disappear under the conqueror's boot.

I lived in Brooklyn. In the Manhattan cafés where refugees gathered and spoke German to one another, the gap between their fortunes in Europe and the miserable employment they could find for the most part in America made their exile tragic. For me, to work as I did in a music shop or a grocery was no hardship. And my patron arranged singing lessons for me; I groomed my hair, spent money on my teeth, and hoped my child would blossom into an American schoolgirl. If I had no opportunity to find a place on the New York stage, I did not grumble at my situation. Lenya had explained to me how little work she had. Weill made his way, and worked with many writers and poets, but Lenya had not yet made a dent on the brassy New York scene, and I accepted that if she could not, I had even less chance.

Then *Lady in the Dark* opened, and everything changed. Kurt was an American success. And suddenly Lenya was wanted too.

2

I cannot remember exactly when I heard Lenya sing again after such a long time. It wasn't on stage. It was probably in the three-storey brownstone house run by George Davis in Brooklyn Heights. Auden had some association with the place, I think, though I never met him there; it was used as a kind of live-in salon, to which Lenya took me one evening. She had a longstanding friendship with Davis, and thought it would do me good to meet a few theatrical people. She had begun to rehearse for a small part in a new show, and she looked once again as vital as she had in her twenties. Prompted by many requests, she agreed to sing.

Her voice surprised me. She had been a good, classical soprano in our Berlin days; now her voice was lower and growlier; more like mine had always been. The young men liked her voice and called out requests, while George Davis put his hand on her knee in an attitude which suggested they were lovers. I watched without astonishment. If they were lovers, it mattered nothing to me. I was interested in the voice, and their approval of that. Perhaps mine too might be liked in this new world.

Then a young boy with a pinched face, who was Czech, I believe, began to talk about Brecht's doings in Santa Monica, and my attention swung to him.

'He will have to write for films. The theatre is hopeless for him here,' said the Czech boy. 'In the serious theatre they are only interested in Stanislavsky and the Method.'

None of them spoke of his poetry or his plays, but somehow their omission to debate his genius made it the more evident for all of us.

'People quarrel with him,' said Lenya. I heard the malice in her voice. She could not forgive the way Brecht had behaved to Weill over *The Threepenny Opera*.

'Still, his sympathies are always with those who are exploited,' I said.

160

They ignored my remark.

Later that night, I taxed Lenya with infidelity to Kurt and she shrugged. 'Sometimes I feel very insecure,' she explained.

'But Kurt?' I asked. 'I thought you needed him so desperately?'

'Well,' she shrugged, and gave me one of her old, wicked grins. 'We are an old married couple now, we understand one another.' And then she told me that Kurt was unfaithful himself occasionally these days, and she found it hard to tolerate, harder than he had found it to tolerate her own indiscretions, she admitted.

That interested me. 'Why should that be?' I asked.

'Sex never went to the root of his being,' she said. 'It was his music first, always, for him. I told you that.'

'And you?'

'Women see themselves so differently,' she said.

I brooded a little on that, as she lit a cigarette and tried to chase away her own gloom. I wasn't sure how I saw myself.

'When there are problems,' she said, 'Kurt and I always stand together.'

It was the kindness of Kurt and Lenya that gave me my New York life. They arranged a musical evening for me under the auspices of the League of Composers at the Cosmopolitan Club on East 66th Street. I was billed as Madame Frieda Bloom, Chanteuse. I was very nervous. Lenya's success could not make me less apprehensive. Would there be room for another singer with a harsh voice to sing ballads in German or with a German accent?

I need not have worried. There were enough German speakers in New York that month to fill the small rooms again and again. Afterwards, one of the young men who had listened so intently to Lenya at George Davis's salon came up to me.

He was a young man with an English style, as I saw it, very elegantly dressed with hair prematurely grey round his unmarked face. Something inaccurate in the first remark I made to him made him laugh, and I flushed at my own clumsiness, and turned away from what I saw as his snobbish amusement. Looking back, I saw he was talking to a group of younger actresses, and I felt angry to see them laughing together, since he kept his eyes on me, and I was convinced he was retailing my clumsy error.

161

As I prepared to leave, I discovered there was a sudden downpour of rain and, hesitating, found him suddenly at my side. 'Let me help you find a taxi,' he said, plunging out into the rain and waving wildly.

'I could go back in and get a friend to take me home,' I said, oddly nervous of him.

But Weill and Lenya had melted away earlier, and I knew no one else I could turn to.

'Be patient, there are always more taxis,' he said.

I smiled ruefully.

'While we wait you can tell me everything that has happened to you,' he said.

'I work in a bookshop in the Village,' I said as flatly as I could.

He laughed. 'Why, you whore of Babylon,' he said lightly. 'And there I was, thinking of you as Frieda Bloom, a cabaret singer from Berlin.'

I laughed at that. A taxi drew into the kerb. He opened the door for me.

That there was something sexual in his invitation I had no doubt, even as he put a courteous hand under my elbow to help me into the taxi. The thought alarmed me. He was young, for all the pale grey hair round his face. And his good looks disturbed me as I stole an uneasy glance at the silhouette of his nose and lips. It was so long since I had felt my breath quicken that it took me a moment to recognize what I felt as desire. I was impatient with myself as soon as I did. Could I be so foolish as to give up my undemanding celibacy? It had brought me much peace.

For a while we sat in silence. The traffic was locked in the rain; the lights flickered on the black streets.

'You look so bold on stage,' he murmured. 'Why do I think if I asked you to come and have a drink with me you would refuse?'

I was amused by his tentative approach, but I did not see why I should help him. Yesterday he would not have turned to look after me in the street. I should have been no more than a woman in middle years, well groomed perhaps, but still a little too sallow, a little too heavy around the eyes. And ten years older than he was. Without my songs he would not have seen me, still less wanted me. I was travelling in the glamour of my stage presence. And yet knowing all this did not diminish the attraction I felt.

'We are passing my flat.' He gestured up at a huge glassy monster. Outside, the rain had become torrential. I rubbed a little space in the misted windows and gazed up at the acres of black glass. Then I put aside my timidity. Life was too short and bleak for cowardice.

'All right,' I said.

The casual words changed my life. With them I began my last and longest love affair with the record producer Maxwell Johnson. I have to say I did not know who he was. I did not know that he owned radio stations; I had no suspicion of his wealth. I had no sense that putting my foot across the threshold of the lift which whisked me up towards his penthouse was the most important step of my life. If I had known, I might not have taken it. I had always been so unlucky in love; it was almost as if pain had been a necessary condiment.

The success I had wanted found me so late in life it might almost have been thought too late, except our reality lies in how we end up. I have seen so many lives end in disaster. So many begin with golden chances, are successful early on and then go downhill all the way. Mine has been a hard life. I missed many things which ordinary women take for granted. Looking at me smouldering at the footlights long ago in Berlin there was always an irony: a shabby fifty-year-old housewife was probably getting more sex than I was. And when at last my voice and face became fashionable in smart New York circles, I received the praise and the money with appropriate gratitude and a certain calm. For the time being I moved from Brooklyn to Manhattan.

I had determined to make no effort to see Brecht while he was in America, but I had not put him altogether out of my mind. Once Brecht came to New York to oversee a German language production of several scenes from *The Private Life of the Master Race*. We had difficulty getting tickets and I wrote a note to the flat where he was staying with Ruth Berlau. I guessed his memory of me would ensure a response. And so it did. When the tickets arrived, I saw Max was watching me closely.

'So,' said Max, 'what will you do? Are you going to be snarled in again?'

'I want to see him,' I admitted.

'Don't let him bully you,' said Max dryly.

I shrugged.

'And don't sleep with him,' he added.

My daughter was now old enough to voice her own dislike at his incursion into our American routine. 'Why can't you just live a normal stable life with Max? You are so happy now. Why all that again?'

'Because I haven't had a normal stable life,' I said. 'You are being coached for exactly that.'

And indeed she was and has found it. It has been a great joy to know as much.

Brecht and I met some time after that production in a New York breakfast café, where he seemed to be enjoying the rye bread. He was gaunt in the face and behind the steel-rimmed glasses his eyes were deeper set than I remembered. I saw too that his lips were tighter, and his teeth even more decayed. He had a two-day growth of beard; and although his hair was still brown there was a balding patch clearly visible.

'It is not easy to be an enemy alien,' he said. 'How do you manage?'

I knew I was looking well, and his eyes going over my face confirmed as much, though what he actually said was rude. 'You look American. I hate that.'

'How are you coping with America?' I asked him.

He laughed. 'In comparison with Hollywood, the little village in Denmark was a world centre,' he said.

He looked around the café where a characteristic group of refugees from Middle Europe was beginning the day almost as late as he was. I guessed Hollywood was treating him badly, but he rebuffed my attempt at concern. 'In America everything is so benevolent,' he said. 'I hate the language. It is a language made for nice guys, which is to say liars.'

I asked him how the studios treated him.

'Wherever I go, they ask me to spell my name,' he said. And he grinned.

'Are you working?' I asked him, seeing the hatred under the grin.

'Work? It is the only commandment I ever recognized,' he said.

'I worked when running away from the Gestapo. Nowadays,' he shrugged, 'I am less productive.'

'Why don't you come to New York?'

'It's cheaper over there. Much cheaper. And there must be at least sixty of us.'

'Us?'

'Émigré German workers, trying to make a buck out of the Hollywood film industry. My entry into the market place has not been a great success,' he said ironically. 'I've been living on less than an unskilled car worker.'

I murmured something, embarrassed, about early difficulties.

'They don't take my ideas,' he muttered. 'I'm only here this week because something I wrote with Feuchtwanger was bought by Goldwyn.'

'I'm sorry. I'm glad. Both,' I said, stupidly.

'I wanted to have a story set in newly liberated France, a heroine who is mistaken for a collaborator. She should have had a shaven head. No actress would do it.'

'How is Helli?' I asked.

'Helli is very good at finding furniture,' he said. 'Furniture from the past. Evidently in the past America was a cultured nation.'

'And does she get any acting parts?'

He stared at me for a while, assessing what had been happening to me. I explained what Lenya and Weill had done for me.

'You are like my old friend Fritz Lang. You give the public what it will accept,' he said with contempt.

I shrugged.

'They want smooth, smart lines,' he said. 'Won't you be ashamed for me to come and see your show?'

'No,' I said. 'It's good.'

And then abruptly he scraped back his chair from the table. 'Helli has no parts. None. It is like being dead.'

After this meeting, Max and I had our only quarrel. He objected to the interest I took in Brecht, not out of jealousy but for a more complex reason, whose justice I had to acknowledge.

'You sit at the edge of his life and look in,' he said simply.

I flared at that, but when my temper had calmed a little, I said reflectively, 'Is it so wicked? To be a voyeur? A spectator? It is one of the roles of an artist, to look on and reflect.'

Then I showed him some of the new songs I had been writing, and when he had read them through he said slowly, 'How calm you have become.'

'I like that,' I said. 'It leaves me reflective. I am happy like this. Happy with you.'

And so I was.

New York shimmered. I don't think I had ever realized from the films how beautiful it was; how sharp and clear the light, how skyscrapers perched like elegant, silver insects above the straight avenues; how brilliant the sky was. To walk along in Manhattan sunshine made me feel free.

Lenya and Weill had moved to a new house, and for a time I lost sight of them, as Lenya was occupied all day with carpenters, plumbers and house painters. One day, soon after this, Max and I called to see them; and Max went off with Kurt to admire the trout stream while I was beckoned to talk to Lenya in the kitchen. Soon Kurt joined us, and I guessed they had been arguing about something.

'Brecht keeps writing to Kurt,' said Lenya. 'He wants to put on an all-black production of *The Threepenny Opera*. In California. He has all kinds of ideas.'

'What does Kurt say?' I asked, as neutrally as possible.

Kurt only smiled. I don't think he wanted to discuss it with anyone. He murmured something about *The Good Woman of Setzuan* and Brecht's unwillingness simply to be a librettist.

'I don't trust Brecht,' said Lenya emphatically. 'Certainly not about financial arrangements and the division of royalties.'

'He went through many unpleasant things,' said Kurt, mildly.

'Not unpleasant enough to change him,' she said. 'You forget things too easily, darling. I remember everything he did to you. Of course he wants to work with you now you are successful.'

'He sounds nicer,' said Kurt.

'When he's down, perhaps. That's natural. But just let him get a bit successful again and he'll be the old Brecht.'

'He's short of money,' I said. Max and I had sent him some that month.

'Kurt could send him 100 dollars,' she suggested.

'I could afford to send him something monthly,' said Kurt.

The whole conversation had affected me strangely. 'Why won't people help him?' I asked.

She laughed. 'He has plenty of helpers. Berlau helps him. And Weigel. She cooks for him.'

'Can't she get work?'

'It's impossible for a German actress.'

My eyebrows rose dumbly. 'Why can't Hollywood make a place for him?'

'He won't write what they want,' said Kurt.

I tried to read that face, polished smooth as it was, and could not do so. 'He doesn't know how to,' I said wearily. For a moment Lenya thought I was criticizing Kurt and I saw a flash of anger in her eyes.

'He's crazy. He makes a theory out of it,' she said.

Some months later I met Brecht again briefly, this time with Weigel in Weill's New York apartment. Everyone was discussing Charles Laughton, because Brecht explained he was the most important person he had met in America.

'He came into our house with a coat over his head,' said Weigel. 'He was embarrassed to be recognized.'

She was now a marvellously handsome woman, like many women whose strong features look better in middle age. Life had lined a quizzical intelligence into her face; I imagined her looking up from a stove as she had in her Berlin apartment, with an upward-looking gaze, and ironic eyebrows, and it came to me suddenly: they are alike, she and Brecht. Like two peasants. How clever they are, cleverer than all of us.

It was only a flash, that vision, because I could not miss her suffering. Her sense of failure was palpable; it made her ashamed, because she was the greatest German actress of our day; and seeing her defeat made me angry too. I caught her eyes as I stared at her, and the amusement in that tough, boned face caught me unawares. She had seen my anger, and understood it. I realized I was angry because she was still at Brecht's side; and that this was not a matter of envy but indignation, because it must have been such an ordeal for her.

'Laughton enjoys the pleasures of his belly,' Brecht said. 'He is ideal for Galileo. I like his belly. He carries it around like a poem.'

167

3

I was with Weill and Lenya when the news came through that the war in Europe had ended.

'It is a miracle,' said Kurt. 'That justice should have defeated evil.'

We had a quiet celebratory dinner, Max, Kurt, Lenya and myself. Max was a good friend to Kurt. He had backed his shows, and offered him friendship long before his American success. And Max and I were friends as much as lovers; I suspect he liked the calmness of our life together; and of course we had a working bond also. I recorded my songs for him. He admired them. I sang to him, and he was proud of me. We had by consent a life in which I kept my own apartment and he kept his. We ate together most nights; he came to my shows when I had them; I listened attentively to his problems; he was concerned about mine.

In an Anglo-Saxon culture, there is always something a little suspicious about attachments to older women, but Max had always felt himself older than his years. It came from the weight of his father's money, the sense that his obligation was to protect and enhance rather than seek protection. He had never been boyish; that premature greying was an outward sign of his own sense of himself. And he knew so much more than I did. In America I was still a child; a daughter, willing to learn.

His family might have frightened me, in the splendour of their New England mansion with their Dutch ancestry and their oil paintings. Luckily Maxwell preferred the raffish world of New York. There we were excellent companions. And he brought an amused tenderness to my daughter.

My daughter was learning English with the speed that only an American environment can ensure; even those long Russian 'O' sounds were disappearing, and it was already clear that she had considerable academic ability. She was ashamed of the outspoken words of my songs, and once I overheard her lying to a school friend about what I did to pay her school fees. I tackled her about that, and she shrugged. 'Showbusiness is the worst of this country.'

'Do you prefer the Soviet Union, then?' I shouted at her, loving her painfully and afraid we were drifting apart.

She smiled, her lips tender and ironic, in a curve that was oddly familiar.

4

Soon after the end of the war, Kurt Weill was dead, at fifty.

At his funeral spring rain fell over the valley. Only a few friends were there; Lenya was white-faced and dazed, as if under sedation. There were flowers in the open casket, and someone said they looked beautiful.

'He is beautiful,' said Lenya, her voice low, her eyes blank. And I reflected with a kind of envy on the long years they had remained together and the pain they had given one another. I'd always liked Kurt, from a distance, without getting very close.

'I'm sorry, I'm sorry,' I said to Lenya after the short ceremony and then suddenly confessed, 'I don't feel I ever knew him well.'

She embraced me then, with the first smile of recognition. 'There was always a wall around Kurt,' she said. 'Nobody knew him. Even after twenty-four years I'm not sure I really knew him.'

Some people are like that, I thought; they exist inside themselves with great power, and make only the gentlest contact with people. And then there were other people who trammelled you with great urgency in every way they could; forcing you to know their intimate thoughts, and not only their thoughts but also their blood pressure, heart rate and inner acidity. Brecht was like that. I frowned to remember as much and wondered if such insistent communications give any greater understanding of the person within.

'What is there to know?' I asked Lenya wearily.

I spoke to Brecht one last time in America; only briefly and in company. Max was a friend of Peter Lorre, who was at that time reduced to pathos through drug dependency, and the misery of being offered only clownish parts. Max had some idea of helping him which involved Brecht, and we all had dinner together at a smart restaurant in Manhattan. I remained calm enough at the prospect of seeing Brecht again. Max watched me closely as I dressed that evening, and I could see he was pleased at my composure.

When we all sat down round the white linen, I knew I was looking my best, although that best was essentially bought with dollars; my hair was groomed, my dress elegant. I had acquired a regal manner to go with the position Max's friendship had given me, so that neither Weigel nor Berlau recognized me at first. When they did, I saw, they instinctively checked with Brecht to read his reactions.

He registered my well-being with a slow smile. In turn I acknowledged to myself that he still had some physical power over me, but I was determined to give no sign of this. Max was watching me, and might well have arranged this dinner with some such test in mind.

I had sent Brecht a book of my songs, translated into English and brought out in a fine edition, and I asked him politely if he had looked at them.

'I have them in German,' he said, patting his heart.

It was the only exchange we had.

I kept my face wooden and courteous, and sat myself as far away from Brecht as I could. I was there to be spectator, and nothing more. So it was I watched the kindness Brecht showed Lorre; observed with irony the dark figures of Berlau and Weigel at his either hand; and reminded myself that I had cut him out of my heart.

There was another reason why I stared at Brecht that night, with peculiar fixity, however, and that was a secret I was keeping to myself. Something I had not let myself consider before. That was because it concerned my daughter.

Her childhood prettiness, when she had so much resembled my sister Minna, had been dispersed by adolescence. Now she was healthier and more American in body. It was natural. Sometimes in her movements she resembled me. But there was something else. These days I couldn't help but make out a resemblance she bore to the boyish Brecht. I wanted to think I was mistaken. I promised myself the probabilities were small. And I spoke of my thoughts to no one, least of all my daughter. She had been shown the gentle, dreamy face of Seryozha as her father; she remembered Itzik as the parent who amused her. Now she accepted Max as her protector. Even if my suspicions were true, and resemblance is an elusive matter, how could I present her with yet another father?

I remember that evening sharply. The discussion at the other end of the table was about *Galileo*; Maxwell was being asked to put up a little money for the production; he sometimes operated as an angel in the theatre. I don't think he decided to become involved, but as I sat silent and watchful, I thought about Brecht and the figure of Galileo.

It was a play I knew he had written several times. The first time was in Denmark with Steffin; she told me about it. He'd been thinking about science and atomic war when he began; then about trials and tyranny. The Moscow show trials were on. The knowledge he had of those events coloured the play. Now he was writing the play again. I watched him as he ate.

Galileo. He was Galileo.

Galileo in all the versions of the play is tainted; venal, and food-loving. It was only the clerical enemies he opposed that made him heroic. And that was true of Brecht also. He had been the enemy of the Nazi butchers; and those friends he had in the United States honoured him for it. There were other points of similarity. Galileo was inventive, rather than original; he took over the work of other men's hands, without scruple, and his own thoughts rested on those of other men. Brecht also. And Galileo too stood not so much for honesty as inquiry. Even as I thought along these lines, I heard Brecht's voice rise with excitement. 'I don't want atmosphere. I don't want mood. I want truth.'

I watched Weigel and made out the tenacity and devotion in her face. I watched Ruth Berlau, who wore her hair softly piled on her head in a bun. There had been rumours of pregnancy, childbirth and madness; I could read none of that in her pretty face. But then I had never known her, and it is hard to read the lives of those we do not know. And I heard Brecht's voice again, louder than before. He was drinking a huge glass of brandy. 'Control is the important thing,' he was saying.

172

He had enjoyed little control over his life, for all his adroit trimming; as much as any of us he had been blown about the world by the forces of twentieth-century madness. I don't want to defend his personal ruthlessness; I am not blind to it; the only difference between a genius and any other unscrupulous person lies in what he can give the world, almost accidentally, and even in pursuit of his own interests.

Some time after that dinner, everyone began to hear about the House Committee of Un-American Activities. I was not among those who were anxious at first, though Max talked about the special closed hearings in Los Angeles. The entertainment business was much threatened but I wasn't much concerned myself, until in September Brecht was summoned to appear before that inquiry.

It was Max who explained to me that Brecht was likely to be in trouble.

'Do they think he is a spy?'

Even as I smiled at the idea, a fleeting glimpse of Brecht going off to see what he could do about exit visas came to my mind. I was once again in the train crossing the muddy plains of central Russia, speculating what he had offered.

'In August they had Eisler on the stand. He didn't mention Brecht's name, but of course they are associated,' said Max quietly.

Then he put his hands on my shoulders and turned me towards him. 'Would you like to be in court?' he asked me. 'I can arrange it.'

I was surprised. 'Aren't the hearings closed?'

'There will be reporters. And newsreel cameramen. We can go as friendly observers, as they call it.'

I hesitated.

'It's important to me as an American,' he explained. 'If people had been braver in Germany, fascism would never have happened.'

'You look like your Puritan ancestors,' I said. 'Of course we must be there.'

It was late October. We spent a weekend with a theatre manager and his actress wife in New England. I remember the beauty of their lawns, the brilliant autumnal trees and the pervasive sense of being caught in a dream. A West Coast newspaper carried lists of more than forty people subpoenaed to appear. They were by no means all men of the Left: I think Walt Disney and Ronald Reagan were among them. But there were nineteen who were thought of as particularly opposed to the Committee's methods. Brecht's name was among these, though he was far from the best known: the screenwriters included some of the highest paid in Hollywood. Max and his friends were glued to the radio daily to hear news of the hearings.

As we walked in that New England sunshine, I saw Max was far more disturbed than I was. Indignation was impossible for me: I could not be sufficiently surprised. Max was aflame with the horror of what was happening in America: someone had been pulled from the court and cited for contempt; others were already in jail. Later, when we heard a shouting match in court between one Hollywood writer and the chairman of the Committee, he clenched his fist and drove it hard into the side of the chesterfield on which we sat. Max had not believed in American injustice; now he was angry. As for me, when we boarded the plane for Washington, I had a sense of moving towards a sequence of actions I had performed in some other time.

I did not yet place the memory.

We arrived in Washington the day before Brecht was due to appear, and stayed at the Grand Sheraton. Over breakfast the next day, Max explained to me the problem of those appearing before the Committee. They could not simply tell the truth. If they admitted they had ever been members of the Communist Party, they would be forced to give the names of others they had known. They would then have either to become informers or be given a citation for contempt. It was for that reason that so many of them pleaded the Fifth Amendment. I absorbed the information thoughtfully. He did not seem yet to have realized that I was myself at risk. That morning I dressed so as to seem invisible.

We arrived in the court room in time to hear that the writer ahead of Brecht had been cited for contempt. The room was packed and silent. Max had reserved our places and we took them in the same hush. I could hear the familiar buzz and turn of newsreel cameras.

What did I feel when Brecht was called to the stand? My heart banged so loudly, I could hardly hear what was being said.

He was neatly dressed in a suit; he looked respectful, co-operative, even helpful; he took an oath in the name of God with a demure expression. When he was offered the services of an interpreter, he accepted without fuss. Then he lit a cigar.

I watched with a dry mouth and cold hands.

I saw he had taken some trouble with his appearance, since he knew better than almost any man alive how images work on a stage. And he must have had a reason for that interpreter: perhaps, I guessed, to give him time to frame his answers. Galileo, I thought. Galileo. It was like a stage, with the Committee a hostile audience.

A single late wasp whirred unexpectedly at my hair, and settled briefly on my sleeve. I brushed it away, thoughtlessly.

Brecht's German was clear and familiar, while the interpreter's voice was so blurred with a heavy accent that the Judge had to bend forward and ask him to repeat answers. Brecht was courteous and precise: when he corrected the Committee on the date of his birth, he seemed chiefly concerned to present the chairman with more accurate information. In the same spirit, Brecht admitted straightforwardly that he had known and worked with Eisler for twenty years. Max, at my side, stirred restlessly; he was worried. He could not see, as I could, that Brecht's diffidence was a superb act of calculation.

I became aware of a pain like a blunt needle thrust into my right hand: the October wasp had stung me before falling to the floor. My attention focused for a moment on the red swelling. I had nothing to put on it and, after a moment's thought, sucked at the injury. Max put his heel on the wasp, frowning.

The chairman was leaning forward now to ask the key question, and everyone waited to hear how Brecht would answer it.

'Have you ever been a member of the Communist Party, Mr Brecht?'

Brecht said, 'Mr Chairman, I have heard my colleagues when

175

they considered this question improper, but I am a guest in this country and do not want to enter any legal argument, so I will answer your question fully, as well as I can. I was not a member and I am not a member of any Communist Party.'

There was an audible gasp at his reply. The chairman, as if uncertain that he had understood correctly, repeated the question. When the answer came back almost identically, there was another little ripple in the hall. Had Brecht lied under oath? Would some Party card, forged or not, be produced to rebut his denial?

By this time my hand was stiff with the sting of the wasp. I was mildly allergic to insect bites, and I could feel my arm throb with the reaction. I knew, of course, that Brecht was speaking nothing but the truth, in that he had never joined any party.

The questioning continued, though the voice was clearly mollified by Brecht's apparent willingness to help.

'I believe you have written plays advocating revolution in society?'

'In Nazi Germany,' he began, 'I advocated the overthrow of Hitler.'

'That does not concern us,' said the chairman. Then he read a line of one of Brecht's poems in English. 'Is that your poem?' he asked.

Brecht had the whole room on his side now, and risked a dry joke. 'No. I wrote another poem in German, and that was rather different.'

There was a little laughter from the spectators. It was the laughter of relief. I shared it. It was no surprise to us at the end when the court declared he had been a good witness and an example to others. And yet, as we stood outside in the corridor and Max looked tenderly at my swollen arm, I knew the story was not over for me.

At the hotel, a doctor gave me an injection for my swollen arm. I was shaking with a slight fever. Max soberly packed our suitcases as I lay on the bed. At length, he asked me cautiously, as if the hotel might have listening ears in its walls: 'That answer, was it smartness or deceit?'

And I explained the answer was at once true, devious and

altogether characteristic. But something else had to be confessed. I was equally vulnerable to such enquiries.

'Have you done anything un-American?' Max asked me then.

'I'm not an American yet,' I said as lightly as I could. Max had chivvied me to take out citizenship papers, but I had been dilatory. I don't know why. 'But I belonged to the Party once. They may question me,' I explained.

He took in what I was saying, and I explained more fully. It wasn't just my time in Russia. That might have been easy enough to justify. But there was the earlier membership of the German Communist Party. I was afraid. I was a small enough catch in myself, but there would be people I had known in the Party. The Committee would find me useful to them. Max listened to me for a time, and then reacted with an explosive fury I had never seen before. 'We'll leave the country,' he said. 'Together. London is a good city. You'll find work. I'll arrange it.'

The next morning we heard that Brecht had left for Europe.

After we returned to New York, I was very ill for two or three days. The doctor said it was an allergic reaction: I believe he called it amphibractic shock. The wasp, he said. But I knew it was a kind of terror.

What was I to do about my daughter, who was so altogether happy in her American world? I could not bear to displace her again. My life had been a history of displacement. I wanted something altogether more ordinary and more stable for her. The thought of leaving her even for a short time hurt me, but I knew it was the only thing to do.

I said my farewells to my daughter in her bedroom. She was dressed in short pyjamas, and looked exactly like any other American girl who was going up to Vassar that year. I was proud of her. I looked at her with love.

'Why are you going,' she asked me. 'They will say you are a spy.'

'I'm not and they won't and it will die down,' I said.

'Shouldn't I come with you?'

'No. Stay here and become American. Why not? It suits you,' I said. 'Max will arrange your college fees.'

'And what if I get married?' she said slowly.

She had a boyfriend and I liked him. 'You're too young,' I exclaimed.

'All I want is an ordinary life,' she said. 'With ordinary love. And not moving from place to place.'

'I know,' I said. My throat hurt as if I had swallowed a plum.

She had become a little short-sighted. In those days she refused to wear glasses because the girls in films always took them off to appear pretty. Even without spectacles the resemblance to Brecht was pronounced.

'Don't read too much,' I said helplessly. 'Enjoy being a student.'

'I like reading, but I don't want to be any kind of writer,' she said firmly. 'Still less part of showbiz. People like your friends only care about their egos. What about you?' she laughed at me. 'Will you go on standing on a stage for ever?'

'Let me tell you what makes me happy,' I said. 'Weather.'

She looked bewildered.

'The changes in the seasons, the different kinds of sky, the trees coming into bud. Sunshine. As long as I have the peace of mind to see these things,' I added.

And for that I only needed Max, and the knowledge of my daughter's welfare.

PART SIX

POST-WAR BERLIN

'You will emerge from the flood
In which we have gone under
Remember
When you speak of our failings
The dark time too
Which you have escaped.'

Brecht: 'To Those Born Later'

1

So it was we moved to London. Displaced again, but not unhappy, since I came to love this old, clumsy city, and Max had that wonderful gift of being happy everywhere. We chose a house near Whitestone Pond where the sky was brilliant and high, and the sun dazzled on the painted houses.

I have not told everything, however. For I saw Brecht one last time.

In Berlin. Just before he died.

I went back to Berlin for the first time in 1954. And perhaps even then one plank remained of my ideological baggage. I still believed the Communists were a bulwark against a revival of Nazi thought in Germany. Strange, how certain ideas take so long to disperse. And so I was happier to be going to East Berlin rather than West, for all the presence of Soviet troops.

The city I knew had been bombed very severely, and there was little left of the Imperial city around the Lustgarten. A few landmarks remained, and some were being restored, including the neo-baroque Domkirche of 1894 that had once looked so out of place. Now it stood in the rubble. The Royal Palace had been demolished. I hardly recognized the Marienkirche. Everywhere I saw the signs of defeat; peeling buildings, collapsing sewage systems, cheap clothes. As I took my heavy brass key from the desk of the Hotel Adlon I remembered another era of glittery dresses, ostrich plumes and men in transsexual gear.

My other ghosts had found their appointed places: Aunt Clara had died in Geneva, safely in her lake house with M. Barbusse. But I never did find out what happened to my father. When some years later I accepted a sum of money in reparation, I did so because it would have pleased him to have something come from his lost bones. I had long forgiven him; and as I walked about Berlin, my childhood rose up in my memory with a kind of gentleness.

In the world outside the hotel there were only shabby people, bewildered, hostile, seeing my foreign clothes and hearing Berlin in my voice. I thought they probably hated me, and I resented that. Where were you when I left? I wondered, looking at the pasty-faced maid wiping the handles in the corridor. It's hardly fair now for you to hate me when I return. But her buttony eyes followed me down the corridor as I looked for the stairs. And I wondered unhappily if hatred is the strongest emotion left in the hearts of those who taste defeat.

I had come to entertain in a small theatre. The theatre I wanted to see was Brecht's. Everyone did.

His genius was acknowledged everywhere by then, and had been ever since Weigel's triumphant tour in *Mother Courage*. His troupe, the Berliner Ensemble, was the one everyone rushed to see. And I too wanted to see what they were doing, he and Weigel, the only survivors of my Berlin years, whose exile had been so much harder than my own.

It was a day of bitter cold. The piles of rubble were covered with a rime of frost, and the potholes were shining with ice. The sun was only visible as a yellow glow, somewhere low in the heavy sky. There was going to be a fall of snow, and I could already taste wisps of it on my lips. My breath hurt me. Everywhere I passed small fires, and people huddling round them, stunned and without much threat; no doubt I had the Russian soldiers who patrolled everywhere in pairs to thank for that. Nevertheless, I felt their eyes on my fur coat and high boots.

When I entered the theatre, a smell of wet oilcloth and paraffin enveloped me. It was warmer than the streets, but not a great deal. A man stopped me, and I showed my British passport (the British had been generous). Then I was waved courteously into the stalls. On stage I saw a man dressed in papal robes, and I heard the end of a scene I remembered well.

It is that scene in *Galileo* when the Pope, in the course of his robing, decided to rescind his earlier decision about not torturing Galileo. 'All that will be unnecessary,' he was saying. 'Do you understand? Just show him the instruments.'

A man standing next to me seemed displeased by what he had

seen. He was wearing a mackintosh, and had a face with a lantern jaw; he spoke German with an accent I could not place.

'We should be doing the classics,' he muttered. 'To help people understand the national strength of the volk.'

In the stalls I made out a cluster of people, crowded around someone on a straight-backed chair facing the stage. It was Brecht.

He was even more thick-set than he had been in New York, with an unhealthy solidity, and the texture of his face was puffy. I have seen flesh of this kind in old people treated with drugs for hypertension. The colour had gone out of his hair, and he looked far older than his years. He was a sick man, clearly; and his eyes looked cloudy and troubled, though they flashed blackly enough when he recognized me.

'Frieda,' he said. 'You have come to sing for us.'

I mentioned the name of the cabaret, in a deprecating voice.

He pulled me to him for an embrace. I could smell the tobacco and sweat and something else, a pungent aroma from other days that brought tears to my eyes.

He saw I was moved and said, 'We are rehearsing one of the songs from the old days. Why don't you sing it for us?'

I hesitated. 'You might not approve of my present style,' I said.

But he held my hand seriously. 'Sing it,' he commanded. 'Any way you do it will be good enough for me.'

So I sang to him, and the people around the audience watched a Western middle-aged woman in a fur coat and high leather boots giving her voice to a corrupt song of another time and another place. He gave me a kiss when I returned to his side.

'Good,' he said. 'Do you have time for supper?'

'I have an hour,' I said.

As we made to leave the theatre, I caught my first glimpse of Weigel, standing with a pencil in her mouth at the harshly lit door of an office. She bowed to me in recognition; an odd, ironic motion. And then she brought out a heavy fur coat for Brecht that had been hanging behind the door. 'You'll need this,' she commanded him.

Without a word, he obeyed her, putting one arm after another into the garment she held out. She gave me a little nod. 'You've learnt a lot. We could even use you here,' she said. 'In small parts.'

This rather grudging approval came from a severe unsmiling face.

Brecht saw my discomfort as he led me into the cold night. 'The theatre is hers,' he explained. 'She handles them better than I can.'

I knew who he meant by 'they'.

'Where shall we go?' I asked.

'Are you very hungry?'

'No,' I said.

'Let's just walk a while then.'

'There is nowhere to walk,' I said, gesturing at the faceless, placeless city all around, lit by scattered oil lamps now and the fires of homeless people.

'Nevertheless,' he said impatiently. 'If we want to talk –'

I caught a glimpse of the man who had been standing next to me at the doors of the theatre, and nodded my understanding. So we walked in a city of wreckage and spoke of many things.

'If you are so watched here,' I asked him, 'why don't you come to the West?'

'I have a place here,' he said, and added with irony, 'The government needs my support.'

'You did not object to the Soviet Union putting down the June revolt?' I asked him.

I had not meant to be so aggressive. It was something the Left in London had made much of, and I was curious to know how he felt. Everyone knew he had written a letter to Ulbricht at the time expressing his support for German socialism. He stopped walking for a moment. I had never seen him look so helpless and unhappy; I had never seen either emotion on his face before. The lines had simply never been in his face to express such emotions. To my astonishment he began rummaging in his pocket with his gloves; at length he pulled off his gloves and found what he wanted with his bare fingers. It was a scrap of paper which he had evidently produced many times before.

I unfolded it and could hardly make it out in the poor light. 'What is it?' I asked stupidly.

'This is the full document. Look. I asked for discussions, which is what the workers wanted. I asked for discussions. It's a copy of the letter I really sent Ulbricht,' he said.

He must have done this many times, I thought, as he repeated what he had said from memory. He was ashamed of what had been made of the letter. And yet the famous sentence in which he reaffirmed his loyalty to the German Communist Party was still there.

'Did you think the workers had right on their side then, last year?' I asked him. 'Did you agree with their demands?'

He frowned. 'Listen,' he said. 'There were agitators. If you were here longer you would feel the Nazism still ready under the surface to break through.'

'How many Nazi sympathizers are there here?' I asked.

'If they had free elections, they would be elected tomorrow,' he said. He smiled. 'It might be simpler to dissolve the people and elect another.'

'Is it hard for you here?' I asked directly.

He shrugged. 'I'm still harassed by the Stasi. Helli arranges everything. And fame protects,' he said with a wry grin.

I folded the piece of paper and he put it back into his wallet carefully. It was important to him that he should not be misjudged by me; I could see as much; and that was also new.

He talked as if it were important to him what I thought. As if I had become a significant witness; or more precisely, as if all witness to his behaviour had become a matter of significance to him. As if he feared judgement.

'One of my students was arrested just the other day,' he said. 'You must understand, we are often criticized here. Naturally . . . since Helli and I spent the war years in America.'

As we walked I could hear his breathing was uncomfortable. 'I saw the workers in that strike,' he said, 'but I also saw some well-dressed people who might well have been *agents provocateurs* from the West. It all reminded me of the last days of Weimar.'

We walked in silence, while my own mind arranged itself about another matter. I knew this was likely to be the last chance I would have to suggest to him that we might share a child. I wanted to make clear that I had never told the child, that I wanted to make no claim on him; that it was a matter of sentiment only, something we could share without disturbing any arrangements he had made. But anything so personal seemed remote and irrelevant to him in the light of his moral preoccupation.

And so I said nothing. After all, I could not be certain.

I have never regretted that silence, which left that last walk of ours so perfect a communion of spirits.

'A wise man is sometimes devious,' he said.

I looked behind him. There was the man in the mackintosh again, with his unmistakable attention.

'I shall win the Lenin prize,' he said. 'I shall thank those who award it as if it were the greatest honour of my life.'

He took my hand, stopped and stared into my face with great intensity. 'I shall die soon,' he said. 'One way or another.'

I protested.

'The doctors warn me so,' he said.

'You have ruined your health,' I said as lightly as I could.

'Brandy and cigars,' he chuckled. 'And women. You were never faithful to me, Frieda.'

'Wasn't I?' I asked unsteadily. I thought about that heart of which I had such a small part.

'Don't cry,' he said to me.

'You always said women cry when they are scolded. That it was a kind of sensuality,' I said.

'And do I still arouse you?' he asked me.

He held both my hands. I felt now all the tenderness of which I was capable and I could say nothing. He saw as much.

'Those of us who tried to do something. Anything,' he said grimly, 'we are the ones at whom all the broken fingers will point afterwards.'

I thought then, and I have thought since, that in the struggle to benefit this poor animal man on our wilderness of a planet there are far greater wrongs to be forgiven than his. And even then, to

186

brood over motivation and intentions misses the point about a man like Brecht. It is only what a man does that can be judged; only his actions that are good or bad; not his motives; nor his state of mind.

'Your poems will stand,' I said strangely. 'Whatever else.'

He seemed to feel what I meant.

We returned to the theatre, and he went in to continue the rehearsal. A girl had been waiting for him, I saw. They exchanged a few words. She was an actress, and I did not have to guess what her relations were with Brecht. She was young, pretty and anxious.

'What is her name?' I asked of someone standing about.

'Kathe,' they said.

When Brecht had gone into the theatre, I called her name, and she came over to me; she recognized me from my performance, and no doubt she guessed my own relationship with Brecht from the softened expression on my face. She looked at me strangely when I asked about Ruth Berlau, whom I had heard was still attached to the theatre.

She shrugged. 'Weigel is the only one he can't do without.'

I nodded.

'And she will survive him,' the girl said quietly.

When the news came of his death, I stood with Max looking out at the sunshine of a pale, English day, and knew that for all I had feared to be impoverished by too much loving, that is not the way human beings are destroyed.

I don't regret the shape of my own life. My work has brought me joy. I never feel lonely now, and rarely sad. In some ways I have been very fortunate. My house is near Whitestone Pond, close to an area of London where several generations of European refugees have made their home. I walk on the Heath with relish in all weathers, and watch the seasons change – today the sunshine is brilliant – and look forward to the visits of grandchildren.